THE SWINDON TO GLOUCESTER LINE

Colin G. Maggs

AMBERLEY

Acknowledgements

Grateful thanks for assistance are due to Kevin Boak, Gloucestershire County Record Office, Gloucester City Library, John Mann, Lionel Padin, Public Record Office, Donald Steggles, D. Viner of the Corinium Museum and L. Walrond of Stroud Museum. Especial thanks are due to Colin Roberts for checking the manuscript.

First published 2009

Amberley Publishing Plc
Cirencester Road, Chalford,
Stroud, Gloucestershire, GL6 8PE

www.amberley-books.com

Copyright © Colin G. Maggs, 2009

The right of Colin G. Maggs to be identified as the
Author of this work has been asserted in accordance with the
Copyrights, Designs and Patents Act 1988.

British Library Cataloguing in Publication Data.
A catalogue record for this book is available from the British Library.

ISBN 978 1 84868 341 9

Typesetting and Origination by Amberley Publishing.
Printed in Great Britain.

Contents

Acknowledgements   2

The Cheltenham & Great Western Union Railway   5

Kemble to Gloucester   18

The Gauge Question   22

Locomotives   26

Steam Railmotors   29

Locomotive Sheds   39

GWR Buses   44

Accidents   46

Description of Route   48

Train Services   136

Possible Future Development   140

Cirencester Branch   141

Tetbury Branch   141

Footplate Trip on an Auto Train   154

Signal Boxes   159

Bibliography   160

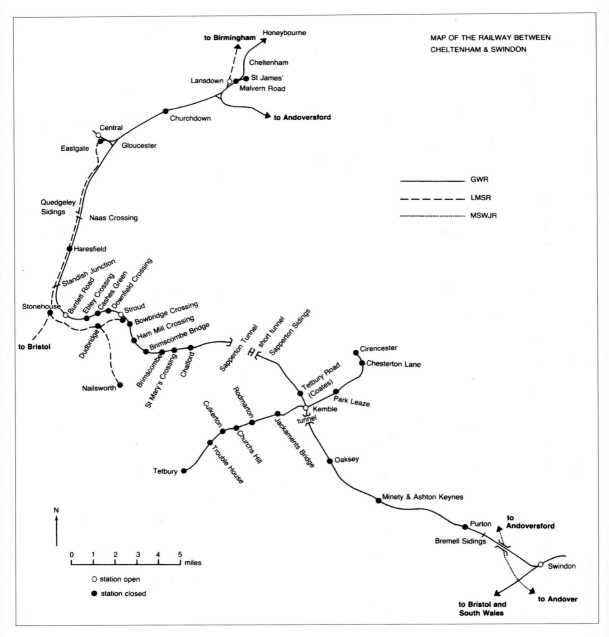

Map of the railway between Cheltenham and Swindon.

The Cheltenham & Great Western Union Railway

The Thames & Severn Canal opened throughout in 1789, allowed inland water transport from Gloucester to London, but was hardly satisfactory due to blockage by ice in winter and shortage of water at the summit level in summer.

On 31 August 1835 the Great Western Railway Act for building a line from London to Bristol received Royal Assent. As this railway was too lengthy an undertaking to be built and opened as one entity, just as happens with today's motorways, it was opened piecemeal. The first section was inaugurated on 4 June 1838 reaching Faringdon Road on 20 July 1840. A wet winter delayed work on the section westwards to Chippenham and the Great Western directors decided that, rather than tolerate delays, they would open the length to a station at Hay Lane, officially Wootton Bassett Road, between Swindon and Wootton Bassett on 17 December 1840. Arrangements were made with the owners of the Bath and Bristol coaches to work between Hay Lane and Bath, the line from Bath to Bristol having been opened the previous August. Gloucester and Cheltenham traffic however continued to use Faringdon Road as a railhead because the highway between Hay Lane and Cirencester was in such a poor state as to be virtually impassable. Swindon station had yet to be opened.

Meanwhile in the autumn of 1833 some enterprising residents of Cheltenham on seeing the Great Western's prospectus, decided to construct a link line. Although as the crow flies only 27 miles separate Cheltenham and Swindon, in order to avoid gradients too steep for locomotive traction, the semicircular line surveyed by Brunel was 44 miles in length and passed through Gloucester and Stroud.

The prospectus of the Cheltenham & Swindon Railway published in 1835 gives the following details:

A Meeting was held at Cheltenham on the 21st of September, attended by Gentlemen from Cheltenham, Gloucester, Stroud, and Cirencester, to consider the expediency of forming a Railroad to connect these towns with the Great Western Railway, at or near Swindon.

It was the unanimous opinion of that Meeting, that the establishment of such a Railway connection would be productive of important advantages to the Agricultural, Manufacturing, and Commercial Classes of the County of Gloucester; and that it should be carried into effect, if it should appear, on investigation, that the probable traffic would pay a fair rate of interest of the capital that would be required.

At that Meeting Mr. Brunel was appointed Engineer, and instructed to survey the Country, and report the most practicable line between Cheltenham and Swindon, and furnish an estimate of the expense; and Messrs Lawrence and Newmarch, and Messrs Griffiths and Pruen were appointed Solicitors, and were instructed to ascertain, and report the probable value of the traffic on the proposed line, against the 3rd of October, to which day the Meeting was adjourned, then to be held at the Tolsey at Gloucester. It was also determined that a Subscription should be opened to defray these preliminary expenses — that, in the event of a Company being formed, such Subscriptions should be taken as payments on account of Shares which might be taken by Subscribers, and that they should be paid into the Bank of Messrs Pitt, Gardner, & Co, of Cheltenham.

On the 3rd of October, the Meeting was held accordingly. Mr. Brunel attended, and reported that an eligible line of Railway could be formed from Cheltenham to Swindon, through the Stroud and Chalford Valley, at an expense not exceeding £750,000.

A beautifully drawn plan with roads tastefully coloured buff and water blue, was deposited in November 1835 for a railway from St James' Square, Cheltenham to the Great Western at Swindon with a triangular junction leading to a station at Gloucester, triangular junctions at Cirencester and Swindon, and tunnels at Chalford and Sapperton. The line was approximately as built except for the last two triangular junctions and the tunnel at Chalford. The surveyor was George Hennet, a similar plan by Brunel being submitted the following September.

Curiously Gloucester showed relatively little interest in the scheme, subscribing only £18,000 compared with the £212,800 by Cheltenham, the £124,900 of Stroud and neighbourhood, and £85,000 of Cirencester. There was certainly a call for a railway. Charles Stephens, owner of a cloth factory at Stroud said that water carriage took too long and was too uncertain, while if goods were carried by road, (23 broad wheel wagons travelled from Stroud and Cirencester to London each week), the bumping over the uneven surface rubbed holes in his bales and although the carriers made good this loss, it was necessarily reflected in their costs. Freight charges from Stroud to London were £5 a ton and London to Stroud £10 a ton, whereas it was anticipated that rail transport would only be £1 16s 0d for the same weight.

A cheese factor at Cirencester said that 3,000 tons of cheese were sent annually from Gloucestershire to London. Road transport cost £4 a ton and the railway promised to do it for only £1 12s 0d. Butter would be sent to London by rail and the facility of rapid transport would be most useful in summer when the excess butter produced in the area around Gloucester deteriorated in the heat, forcing farmers to sell it as grease.

A bird's eye view of New Swindon *c.* 1850. The works complex is to the left and the GWR housing estate and St Mark's church to the right. The line to Gloucester runs behind the works. Author's collection

View west from the passenger station towards the works *c.* 1850; the line to Gloucester curves right. On the left a van has been moved to a siding by means of a wagon turntable. George Measom

Difficulties were met transporting corn by water: if travelling in uncovered coal boats it became damp, as it did when carried in uncovered salt boats. Additionally, corn was pilfered by boatmen, proverbial for their dishonesty, whereas theft was unlikely during the few hours of rail transit. Transport costs for flour sent by road from Stroud to Gloucester were 13*s* 6*d* a ton, whereas the railway promised to charge only 8*s* 0*d*.

Stage coaches took a day to reach London, but by rail passengers would be able to go up and back in a day. The proposed railway was estimated to be profitable. It was believed that counting nine passengers to every four-horse coach, six to every two-horse coach and five to the Mail and by doubling the number of passengers, as opening a railway always brought in increase, 2*d* per head/mile would raise an income of £83,673 4*s* 0*d*. With merchandise bringing in an estimated £16,229 8*s* 0*d* and parcels a further £8,530 12*s* 0*d* the total income was reckoned to be £108,433 4*s* 0*d* giving a return of 7½ per cent on the capital.

Although most folk were in favour of the railway scheme, the vested interests of some parties aroused opposition, the main antagonists being the proprietors of the Thames & Severn Canal which felt its trade threatened by the proposed line, and Squire Gordon of Kemble who did not wish his property to be defiled by a railway cutting through it. Although one may think this opposition petty, a modern parallel would be a threat of a motorway being cut through your land. Both contestants were pacified by a gift of £7,500 each. Gordon urged his claim for immediate payment of the sum, whereas the railway said it would pay when the land was needed. He claimed that he should be put on the same footing as the Thames & Severn Canal, but the Cheltenham & Great Western Union Railway (CGWUR) said that the cases were not parallel. A compromise was reached; in the event of the £7,500 being payable, that is, if and when the railway required his land, Gordon would receive 4 per cent interest on the sum from 21 September 1836.

In May 1838 a further agreement was made with him, a £3,500 bond being payable on 22 June 1838, £2,000 on 11 December 1838 plus 5 per cent interest from 22 June; and £2,000 on 22 June 1839, plus 5 per cent interest from 22 June 1838. On 12 November 1838 Brunel wrote a letter to Lawrence illuminating the squabble with Gordon:

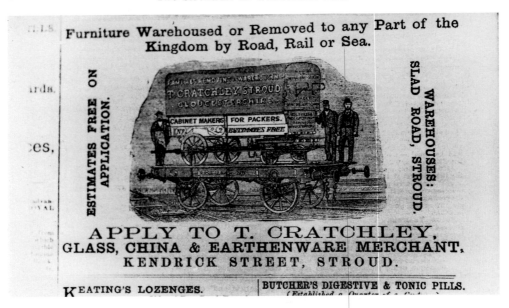

An advertisement in the *Stroud Journal* 27 February 1886 depicting a pantechnicon — an early road-rail vehicle, its small wheels enabling it to be within the loading gauge. Author's collection

. . . there must be one or two conditions insisted upon which must not be yielded on any consideration . . . Pray beg the Directors to be positive and unyielding with Gordon . . . I send you the specification of the Sapperton Tunnel Contracts and one of the drawings which Richardson left behind last night by mistake. I perceive Mr. Gordon's object in attending the Board to take advantage of some chance omissions . . . **One man has always the advantage over a number** *. . . if he is cunning which Gordon certainly is — he seems to be really savage with you.*

Even after the line had been opened, Gordon was still a thorn in the Great Western's flesh, a complaint being received from him that engine noise caused a nuisance at Kemble House. The GWR arranged for *Lion*, a Sharp, Roberts & Co. 2–2–2 built in 1838, to let off steam at 4.45 p.m. on 27 June 1842. The company's solicitors, Robert Brown and Henry Zachary positioning themselves at Kemble House, reported that although the wind was blowing from the station, the noise of escaping steam could only just be heard outside and not at all from the interior of the building.

The Cheltenham & Great Western Union Railway Act of 21 June 1836, 6 & 7 Wm 4 c 77 authorised the construction of a line from Cheltenham to Swindon together with a branch from Kemble to Cirencester with a capital of £750,000 and £250,000 borrowing powers. The Act contained a clause whereby the line would be carried through Gordon's grounds in a tunnel where only a shallow cutting was really required. We tend to think that care of the environment is a modern concept, but Squire Gordon saw that it was written into the CGWUR Act that the company should plant the virgin cuttings and embankments: *. . . in an ornamental manner with good and sufficient shrubs and forest trees, and shall at all times thereafter maintain the said plantations and it shall be lawful for the said Robert Gordon, his heirs, or assigns, or the owners for the time being of the said estate at all times thereafter to enter into and* *upon the said cuttings and embankments and the plantations thereon for the purpose of pruning or cutting and improving and keeping the said plantations in good order, but so as not to impede or interfere with the proper use and maintenance of the said railway.*

No public station was to be built on his estate or within 50 yards of his boundary without his consent in writing.

Initially the Thames & Severn Canal did quite well out of the railway, having spent only £1,068 4s 10d in opposing the CGWUR bill, the railway paid £2,500 cash and £5,000 spread over four-and-a-half years and the canal carried much of the railway's building material. However, once the line was opened it was a different story. The railway took much of the canal's trade and the latter was forced to cut its tolls.

On 28 June 1836, a week after the Act had been passed, Messrs Pitt, Gardner & Co. were appointed treasurers, but the appointment had to be rescinded a fortnight later. This was because Parliament had stipulated that the post should be held by individuals, so on 27 July William Pitt of Cheltenham, Joseph Watts of Stroud and Frederick Cripps of Cirencester were appointed treasurers. It was also arranged that the monthly directors' meetings would be held in rotation at Cheltenham, Stroud and Cirencester. In July the minutes read: 'Brunel to lay down line [ie mark out the line] as soon as the corn is harvested and works will be commenced as soon as the steps taken'. William Henry Hyett was appointed the company's chairman.

By 3 May 1837 contracts had been let for works from Cheltenham to Gloucester and for a considerable distance towards Stroud, while the preliminary shafts of Sapperton Tunnel had been carried to a considerable depth and an examination of the strata had proved that it was more conducive to excavate than had been anticipated. The strata of cuttings had also been explored. At the meeting on 3 November 1837, it was announced that no material progress had been made due to a slump and calls were in arrears on a significant number of shares. Lord Moreton invitied those living in the district to take as many shares as they could and buy them to pay calls, not just for speculation, hoping to sell them at a higher price 'but with the intention of lending the best possible assistance to carry on the undertaking to a speedy and successful termination'.

Apart from Gordon's land at Kemble, most property had been purchased 'on very favourable terms', though between Gloucester and Cheltenham the directors had found it necessary to appeal to Jury for land purchase. In one case the Jury awarded £1,056 for a claim from the landowner of £2,202. In the second case the claim was in precisely the same proportion to the value, the party submitted to the same rate of compensation as had been awarded in the first, without proceeding to the inquiry.

Many shareholders wanted a portion of the line to be completed in order to see a return on capital and considered that Cheltenham to Gloucester would prove the most profitable. The directors argued that Swindon to Cirencester would be better as no less than ten turnpike roads met at Cirencester and such a line would yield an immediate and ample return for the outlay. They backed up this statement by quoting current takings:

Stage coach, 16 miles at 2½d mile	£85,823 11s 0d	=	14,306 passengers
Post chaise	£23,298 4s 2d	=	3,384 passengers
Gigs	£7,120 2s 8d	=	1,187 passengers

Double this number would be expected when the railway was open. The estimated cost of this length was £249,500 and the net income estimated at £25,000.

The directors said that only three wagons ran weekly between Cheltenham and London and two of these ran via Cirencester in order to collect an economic load. Yet from Cirencester 18 to 20 wagons ran weekly carrying 4½ tons each and many 1 ton, or 1½ tons overload. Even at 4 tons each this would bring in £31,200 annually against £4,300 from Cheltenham.

In order to avoid an outlay on purchasing locomotives and rolling stock, on 28 September 1837 the directors made a conditional arrangement for the Great Western to take the completed Swindon to Cirencester section of the CGWUR on a short lease at an annual rent of £17,000, this being confirmed by a seven year lease dated 16 April 1841 giving a satisfactory return on the call up of £35 per share.

On the 22 August 1837 Brunel was instructed to set out the line from Cirencester to Swindon and two contracts were advertised from Cirencester to Minety, while the contract from Minety to Purton was ready six months later. The advertisement for the contract to Swindon was held to await the decision of the Great Western directors to see whether they accepted the deviation for which an Act was passed in 1837, while a bill was currently in Parliament for a deviation from near Frampton the object of saving money by shortening Sapperton Tunnel and getting rid of an 'objectionable' curve, but in doing so, increasing the ruling gradient from a reasonable 1 in 330 to a rather severe 1 in 60. This was authorised by 1 & 2 Vic c 24 of 11 June 1838, which also gave an extension of two years for completion to 21 June 1845 and allowed the Bristol & Gloucester Railway to build Gloucester station if it was not completed by 24 June 1840, though giving the CGWUR powers of repurchase.

Charles Richardson, later to design and make the first cricket bat with a spliced cane handle, though being first and foremost famous as chief engineer to the Severn Tunnel project, was appointed resident engineer of the Swindon to Cirencester section of the CGWUR. The directors decided that the best situation for Cirencester station was 'in the [potato] garden of Lord Bathurst, adjoining the Tetbury Road', the nobleman imposing a condition that the company should 'secure the occupation of a certain house, called the "Castle", opposite the proposed Depot, or contiguous thereto, so as to protect Lord Bathurst from the establishment of an hotel at the point to overlook his park'. Lord Bathurst supported the railway, charging only £200 an acre for the station land compared with the £250 required by Gordon.

In May 1838 the directors criticised the surveying expenses, the principal surveyor being employed for 53 days at an equivalent of £1,000 per annum, and an assistant for 734 days at a salary of £700 yearly, excluding travelling and other expenses. The directors were also justified in criticising Brunel's inefficiency, he having advertised that contracts would be let on 13 June, yet plans and specifications were unavailable even though he had advertised that they were available on 21 May. Charles Frederick Sage of Gloucester was elected acting chairman of the company on 21 August, and since it appeared useless for the directors to try and contact Brunel by letter, one of Sage's first steps was a promise to have a personal interview with him 'and ascertain distinctly from him whether he feels himself really in a situation to carry on the duties of Engineer of the Company'.

Brunel managed to pacify the directors, but two-and-a-half years later they had reason to criticise him again, the minutes recording:

The Directors also especially call Mr. Brunel's attention to the importance of his answering the letters addressed to him by the Secretary under the orders of the Board, when circumstances may not allow of his keeping appointments made with them, which would at least prevent their being called from their homes unnecessarily and the disturbance of the appointments of many persons, whose engagements, Mr. Brunel's own experience will have taught him, are of great importance to individuals.'

In November 1838 all land, except that of Squire Gordon, had been purchased 'on favourable terms' and contractors had started work: Messrs Carter & Spillard holding Contract No. 1 for £15,500; Beaty & Bailey No. 2 for £49,000 and Messrs Oldham of Swindon Nos 3 & 4 for £27,732 and £14,000. The latter began work in February 1839 and it is recorded that he used at least three locomotives, *The Excavator*, *Volcano* and *Vista*, the *Cheltenham Looker-On* for 13 July 1839 reporting:

Unfashionable arrival! On Tuesday last, at noon, the first Locomotive Railway Engine ever seen in Cheltenham, made its appearance in High Street, exciting considerable attention as it passed along, drawn by twelve horses, on a carriage apparently prepared for that special purpose. The lustrous stranger was conveyed along the Promenade and through the new opening near the Queen's Hotel, into the Old Well Lane, and thence to the railway of the Cheltenham and Great Western Union, at the end of Lansdown Place. This engine has been provided by the contractor, Mr Oldham, for the purpose of more rapidly and effectually proceeding with the works along the line, upon which it is to be expected to be in full operation on Monday, commencing its leviathan labours about two miles from the proposed depot [station]. We observe it was very appropriately named 'The Excavator', and have been informed its weight is between eleven and twelve tons.

In 1839 the only work carried out between Kemble and Gloucester was the sinking of five shafts for Sapperton Tunnel. Company shares were at a heavy discount and by the end of the year only £200,000 had been received on calls and arrears amounted to over £40,000. 'Considerable progress' was made on the rest of the line, but then on 30 April 1840 it was announced that 'Four months of incessant rains have occurred since the last meeting and although most cuttings and embankments stood remarkably well, a few had slipped'. In the summer of 1840 Hyett resigned the chairmanship and was succeeded by his deputy Henry Norwood Trye, of Leckhampton Court and a quarry owner. He retired on 2 March 1841 and was succeeded by Charles William Sage. On 10 December the directors expressed disappointment at the slow progress of works which Brunel attributed to slips 'and a want of exertion on the part of the Contractors'. 25 March was fixed for the opening and Messrs Oldham ordered to finish the works by 15 March. In January the overbridge at Purton collapsed; fortunately the sound of its cracking before actually failing, gave men working under it sufficient warning to escape, but 'A man with his cart and horses, however, had scarcely passed over the crown of the bridge before it fell'. The failure was attributed to it being built in frosty weather. The planned date of opening had to be postponed due to an embankment slipping at Purton. It was discovered that its core was saturated and in consequence had in one place subsided 8 feet in 24 hours, while in another had forced in the side of a cottage. The trouble was compounded by the fact that Kimmeridge clay had been dug out on each side to form the embankment and that these longitudinal pits became filled with water during the winter of 1840-1 thus undermining the embankment. Oldham filled the gap at the rate of 1800 — 1900 cubic yards of material each day. Apart from the delay caused in repairing the slip itself, the stoppage of ballast which was originally to have been brought from the other side of the slip slowed ballasting and the completion of the permanent way on the other parts. As all the slips were on the east side of the line, it was decided to lay the permanent way on the western side only and work both ways over the Down line until the slips were cured. On 18 April the Board of Trade was informed that the line was complete and ready for inspection and, reading between the lines, one can see that the directors hoped that the line would be open before the company's general meeting on 4 May 1841 and thus avoid criticism. The inspection train provided for Sir Frederick Smith was drawn by *Venus*, a Charles Tayleur & Co. 2–2–2 built in 1838 and later renamed *Venus No. 1* to avoid confusion with the 'Fire Fly' class engine of the same name. Sir Frederick's report read:

The Act for this line passed in the year 1836 and the works commenced in 1836. Its total length is 36 miles from the junction with the Great Western, at Swindon, at its junction with that portion of the Cheltenham & Great Western Railway which is completed between Gloucester and Cheltenham, and which from being in connection with the Gloucester & Birmingham Railway is worked by that Company.

The works are forming by the Cheltenham & Great Western Union Railway Company under the Direction of Mr. Brunel, and, under an agreement recently entered into, the line in proportion as it may be finished will be leased to the Great Western Railway Company. That part of it which I have inspected is 13½ miles in length of double line, with a Branch of 4 miles of Single line to Cirencester.

The Gauge of this Railway is the same as that of the Great Western, viz 7 feet, and the bearing is longitudinal and continuous. The weight of the rails varies from 54 to 60 lbs and they are rolled so as to present a bevel surface and thus supersede the "canting" of the timbers. The characteristic Gradient is 16 feet in a mile and the steepest Gradient 17 feet in a mile.

The deepest cutting in that part of the line which I inspected is 40 feet in clay, to which slopes of two to one have been given.

The highest embankment in the main Line is 28 feet and on the Branch 38 feet.

The opening of this Railway like that of the Extension of the Great Western from Hay Lane, has been retarded by the slipping of an Embankment composed of clay and formed during very wet weather in the course of the winter before last.

This embankment is near the Swindon Junction and it is a singular fact that subsidence has even amounted to 8 feet in the course of 24 hours. It now however seems to be tolerably firm and as an immense mass of dry and hard material has been brought to the spot, and, by being thrown on the top, has gradually displaced the treacherous material used in the first instance, there is reason to presume that this work will now remain tolerably firm. It will however require careful watching in the course of the approaching winter. The Station at Cirencester will afford sufficient accommodation to the Public as well as to the intermediate stations at Minety and Purton, the latter of which is not finished.

I am not aware of any deviation from the Act of Parliament of sufficient moment to bring under your notice.

The Mile posts are up and the Fences in good order.

There are two crossings of Parish Roads on the level, for which suitable Gates are to forthwith provided.

The Cuttings and Embankments, with the exception of the Slip at Swindon, are in excellent order, and the permanent Way only seemed to require additonal ballast to put it in a good condition.

Mr Brunel has devoted much attention to the mode of forming the junction at Swindon, which he has had arranged with much judgement, with a view to the safety of the passengers. I shall avail myself of the opportunity of bringing under your notice the arrangements at this junction, when I lay before you a general Report on the various Junctions and Stations on the Several Railways in the Kingdom.

At the general meeting it was announced that opening would be on 31 May 1841, but since the goods stations would be incomplete, the Great Western's rental would be reduced. The directors insured Cirencester station for £4,000 and that at Minety for £500 with the Phoenix Life Fire Office. Cirencester had a train shed and a three-storey block, the upper floors including living accommodation. This number of storeys was rare in a small station.

The CGWUR opened to Cirencester on 31 May 1841 and the town, instead of being at the end of a branch off the Cheltenham line, found itself temporarily having the main station. Following the arrival of the *Era* coach from Cheltenham, the first train left at 7.15 a.m. drawn by *Lion*, a Sharp, Roberts 2–2–2, reaching Swindon at 8.05 a.m. and after waiting there for about 10 minutes many of the passengers returned merely having gone for the joy ride. Those that went on to London were hauled by *Greyhound*, a 'Fire Fly' class 2–2–2, and arrived in the capital at 11.02. The *Gloucestershire Chronicle* of 5 June 1841 reported:

Considerable anxiety was felt by an immense number of persons for the coming of Monday last, the time named for the opening of the line from Swindon to Cirencester; this was evinced by the continual flocking together of persons from the town and neighbourhood as often as the train went out or came in. A very beautiful day gave many thousands the opportunity of viewing a railway train for the first time, and their curiosity was satisfied to the full. Many were afraid to approach the engine, but anxious to obtain a full insight as to its construction fixed themselves in some conspicuous and prominent part to view this surprising affair, until every bridge or eminence whether over the deep cutting or on the raised ground was literally covered with observers and their curiosity was amply gratified.

The first train started at a quarter past seven o'clock and reached Swindon at seven minutes past eight. At this point the distance is only 77 miles from London.

Since the opening the trains have been filled as well as might have been expected, but owing to some alterations of management the trains do not keep the regulations first announced in the bills. We are happy to find that not a single accident happened during the day of opening, though something unpleasant might have been expected

Cirencester station *c.* 1850. The train shed, later removed, is to the right of the station building. Author's collection

ESTERSHIRE.
AUCTION,
E and SON,
COLEFORD, on Friday, 18th
on, subject to conditions to be

VELLING HOUSE, oc-
two Cottages, with a Gar-
whose tenancy ends 25th De-
lied with water.
DOWS adjoining the same,
tion of Mr. Thomas Morgan,
d, on completion of the pur-

uarter of a mile of Coleford,
adjoining the new Hampton
n its contiguity to markets is
an, who would find a good

s Morgan, Old White Hart
Ir. T. Gabb, Solicitor, Aber-
the Auctioneers, all of Cole-

SHIRE.
nded Investment.
BLIC AUCTION,
E and SON,
h of St. Briavels, in the
sday, the 15th day of June,
on, under the directions con-
nt of the late Mr. Richard
ch conditions of sale as will

are well supplied with water, and might easily be converted into any establishment requiring room.

For particulars, apply to Mr. Maskelyne, Solicitor, Tetbury, Gloucestershire; or to the Auctioneer, Cirencester.

Tetbury, May 28th, 1841.

CIRENCESTER.
To RAILWAY CONTRACTORS, IRON FOUNDERS, BLACKSMITHS, and Others.
TO BE SOLD BY AUCTION,
By Mr. JEFFERIES,

By order of the Assignees of Messrs. RITSON and CARTER, in a FIELD near the RAILWAY STATION, and close adjoining the Line, on Wednesday, the 16th day of June, 1841 ;—

THE whole of the valuable RAILWAY MATERIALS, BLACKSMITHS' TOOLS, &c. taken from the Works Nos. 1 and 2, on the Cheltenham and Great Western Union Railway ; comprehending more particularly about 60 muck waggons, 200 tons of rails, 1600 feet of 1¼ inch square wrought iron bars, cast iron crossings, lot of pedestals and chairs, horse mangers, bridge centreings, pine timber, about 5000 sleepers, wheeling planks, about 40 wheelbarrows, set of well-sinking tackle and 3 buckets, black-smiths' forge bellows, anvil and blocks, vices, hand-drills, sledges and hammers, a pug mill, quantity of old metal, &c. Catalogues of which will be ready for delivery in due time, at all the principal Inns in the neighbourhood, at the *Midland Counties Herald* Office, Birmingham ; at *Felix Farley's Bristol Journal* Office ; at Smith's Printing Office, and at the Auctioneer's, Cirencester. May be viewed any time previous to the sale, which will begin in the morning, at twelve o'clock punctually.

In the parish of LECKHAMPTON, close to Cheltenham, on the Turnpike-Road to Bath and Gloucester, let at Rents, and of the value of about £200 per annum.
TO BE SOLD BY AUCTION,
By Mr. HOGGART,

the Teeth with ease ; and
let its Gums be rubbed wit
four months, the Syrup
rents should never be with
are young children ; for i
the Gums, the Syrup im
Convulsions, Fevers, &c.

The great success of
Years has induced unpri
name of American Soot
Johnson's Bills, &c. Pa
to ask for JOHNSON's
to notice that the Names
Street, London, (to whom
the Stamp affixed to each
Sold by Mr. D. M. W
able Medicine Venders.

Snook's A
A Most excellent
COMPLAINTS, I
PETITE, HEAD ACHE,
COSTIVENESS, &c.—Th
not contain any Antimon
do not require the least c
exercise promotes their g
or twelve hours after t
worms, purify the hum
remove most complaints
becoming a restorative a
to those of a costive habi
The Pills are now p
(who have purchased th
are engraved on the Gov
out which they cannot b
WALKER, Printer of th

Announcement in the *Gloucester Journal* 5 June 1841 of the contractor's sale of equipment on completion of the line to Cirencester.

from the immense number of persons that passed through the station and witnessed the starting of the train from the covered way. We have no hesitation in saying that many thousands of persons on that day paid a visit to the Line.

The civility of the persons upon the establishment at the station (a very chaste and elegant building) was very pleasing to the visitors. The arrangements at the station were when complete very commodious, and the excellent arrangement of the incoming line of rails prevented confusion in the arrivals and departures. The Company have certainly shown every attention to the comfort and convenience of their customers, and we must not omit to mention their providing a waiting-room where parties may remain that are waiting for the incoming train, provided with every necessary for warmth and comfort during the winter months. We do not find any provision for refreshment room, and we hope some satisfactory arrangement may be made to enable passengers requiring refreshment to obtain it. We observe the effect of this opening upon Cheltenham will be to alter the arrangements of the mail department, and receive notices calling upon persons willing to contract for the conveyance of the mails from Cheltenham to Cirencester and from Northleach, etc., in spring carts or by horse, to lodge estimates. The alteration takes place properly on the 25th June or the next 5th July.

Takings for the first week amounted to over £100 daily from first and second class passengers, while 'In addition to this a very large traffic in goods and third class passengers has taken place.'

Soon after opening the embankment began to slip again. As it occurred chiefly on the east side, the Down line could be kept for two way traffic using a pilot engine, the Up line being used for permanent way trains bringing repair material. By the autumn the Up line had subsided several feet below the Down. Early in December a worried traveller from Cheltenham wrote to the Board of Trade:

I returned by the railway, and as far as Swindon all was very well, notwithstanding the wet, but from Swindon to Cirencester I was horrified at seeing the road I was passing over, and nothing shall tempt me to do it again. One line of rails has slipped for a mile or two completely away and the trains travel on the other line, which appears just hanging by a thread, and this on a precipice of 40 to 50 feet.

Such a letter could not be filed away without some action being taken, so General Pasley carried out a thorough inspection in January, found that facts had been exaggerated and reported:

Fortunately the ground on the western side of the embankment remained firm, so that the slips took place on the eastern side only, where the clay, almost in a fluid state, gave way and moved towards the adjacent cutting, this movement taking place below the surface, as was proved by the remarkable fact that some very strong piles, which had been driven at the bottom of the embankment, were forced forward out of their original line, moving along with the clay; and in one part in particular some of them are now to be 70 feet in advance of their former position. This movement was described to me as having been very slow, so that if carefully watched, and men stationed to stop the trains, no danger can arise from it; but it was so powerful on the east side that the ground under the rails there sank no less than three feet in 24 hours in the worst part.

To make good the embankment Mr Brunel has caused soil of a better quality to be brought from a hill at the north end of it, and to be continually laid on the east side, using the rails on that side for the transport of this earth; and, having found piling to be of little use, he has directed a dry wall of rubble stone, 12 feet thick, to be built at the bottom of the slope to the depth of ten feet, which is equal to that of the cutting, as a retaining wall, to prevent further movement at the base of his embankment towards the ditch or deep cutting on that side; which, as a further precaution, he has ordered to be filled up opposite to those places where the greatest movement of the moist clay took place. These measures will, no doubt, prove effectual, for, as I said before, the western line of rails is perfect throughout, and the eastern line is now only about 15 inches lower than the other in the worst part, and is being gradually brought up to its proper level, which Mr Brunel hopes to accomplish in four or five weeks.

Richardson, the line's resident engineer, in addressing the Geological & Engineering Sections of the British Naturalists' Society in May 1891 gives us an insight of how the work was carried out:

The largest of the slips was about 110 yards in length; breaking away on top, from near the middle of the bank, and, at bottom, carrying forward the recess (or 'cess' as the men called it) at the foot of the bank along with them. The clay was, in fact, sliding back into the side-cutting from which it had been dug. The 'cess' preserved its level, but was shoved gradually forward fastest in the central parts, and more and more slowly towards the end.

Slips always form a conchoidal 'slipping surface', nicely lubricated, and as smooth and polished as the inside of a marine shell, on which the mass slides slowly downwards. By digging down into the slip this 'slipping surface' is readily detected, the material naturally breaking away from it. Its form is always conchoidal; starting from a nearly upright face on top, it forms a graceful curve down to a nearly level surface at the bottom.

To stop these slips, Brunel, after inspecting them carefully, made up his mind to drive a row of strong piles along the 'cess' as rapidly as possible. He sent down half a dozen pile engines with 30-cwt. monkeys, and piles were obtained from beech trees in the woods in the neighbourhood of Chalford Valley. These were cut into piles not less than ten inches diameter, and twenty-feet lengths. Everything was on the ground in three or four days. The 'cess' made a capital floor for the pile engines to stand upon; the piles went easily through this plastic clay, each engine being able to drive ten or a dozen piles in the day; and in less than a couple of days all the piles upon a 100-yards slip were driven in a row. But the slip took no notice of them, and the pile-heads, which stood up a foot or so above the ground, kept on advancing along with the 'cess', but with an increasing prominence of curvature in the centre.

The idea of pinning down the 'cess' to the ground below, which was not moving, and so stopping the advance of the slip, was so obvious that it was natural that piles should be the first thing tried, and everybody was surprised when they entirely failed to produce any effect.

The slip advanced at a speed of about an inch an hour, a rate of movement imperceptible to the eye, yet it progressed with such force as to shear off the green beech piles at the slipping surface, ten feet below the 'cess' without the smallest apparent check. The piles had, I knew, gone into the <u>sound</u> ground below the slip to a depth of eight feet; and how could that soft clay form a cutting wedge by which to shear off the tough stringy green beech piles? Afterthought, however, convinced me that this power was given to the clay by the enormous weight of the superincumbent load, about 200 tons upon each pile. I afterwards drew a good many of the piles and found that they had been torn clean across the 'slipping surface,' a ragged, fibrous fracture showing the toughness of the timber.

Two miles to the north of this big bank we had a short rock-cutting in the coral-rag formation, and I had been thinking out another plan — viz., to dig holes, each six feet square and six feet apart, in the 'cess' — close up to the slope of the bank; to carry them down to a depth of a foot or eighteen inches below the 'slipping surface' into the unmoved ground below, and then to fill these holes with the rough stone from the coral-rag. As it was of the greatest importance to get these holes excavated and then filled with stone as rapidly as possible — for the holes themselves would greatly weaken the resistance of the foot of the slip while they were open — I had only the alternative holes dug first, intending to put down the intermediate ones afterwards. I had a train of waggons full of stone ready, and the holes were filled simultaneously. In digging the holes a novel plan was adopted. Though the stuff was a nice grafting clay, yet the grafting tool is very heavy, and a navvy can only cast his graft to the height of his shoulder, about five feet, say; and to get down twelve feet he would have to get two stages on which to cast the grafts, rendering the process slow. I therefore put one stout navvy with his grafting tool into each hole, and a young active countryman equipped with a short-handed pitchfork with him. The navvy had only to turn the grafts over; then the countryman stuck in his pitchfork (a comparatively light tool) and flung the clod over his left shoulder. This they were able to do comfortably and with remarkable celerity from the bottom of the hole, the navvy taking rather lighter grafts when the hole was deep. The work thus went on with remarkable speed. The effect was immediate, and, in its extent, unexpected, for although in explaining my plan to Brunel, I had insisted upon the important effect of the rough stones, if dragged along the slip, roughening up the smooth and glossy surface of the 'cess', and causing soon so much friction as to stop its progress, I did not feel able to form any definite opinion as to the immediate resistance of a pile of loose stones against the enormous pressure of the slip, as proved by the simultaenous shearing of the beeches. All the force of the slip, however, could not move the counterforts in the least — it was stopped dead, and at once, as I had the means of knowing by marked pegs which I had driven for the purpose of exacting measurement of its progress. The alternative holes were never put down.

The effect of this extremely sudden check to the motion of the slip on the east side, while under full way, appeared to be, as by a sort of rebound, the starting of a similar slip on the west side of the bank, exactly opposite. As the west side had to carry the single line then open for traffic, and this west side slip went down four or five times as fast as the other, it caused great trouble and excitement. Brunel, determined to keep the traffic going, arranged for train-loads of sand from Swindon to be brought there, between the passenger trains, and cast out by a crowd of men to keep the working line constantly raised. But the slip went down still faster; so the line was raised by placing beds of faggots, close together under the sleepers, and then tipping sand over the faggots to steady them.

I was on the bank night and day during the worst time, and saw the trains over. We sometimes lifted the rails quite three feet between two trains, packing the faggots under the train, and then tipping the sand among the faggots. It was a 'broad gauge' line with longitudinal sleepers, otherwise it could not have been kept safe for the trains, and I took particular care to have the rails in a straight line, well to gauge and level across.

We could not keep the road up to its proper level, and at the worst times it was eight or nine feet below the level in the middle of the slip; but I eased off the gradients at the ends to make them less steep, and in this condition the trains took passengers across for many days, until we succeeded in checking the progress of the slip by appliances at its foot. In the meantime, however, the descent the trains had to go down was fearful, and most of the engine-drivers went at it so timidly that I was afraid that they would never get up the rise again on the other side. There was one man, a very plucky driver, Jack Hurst, whom the other men nicknamed 'Hell-fire Jack.' He always looked for me when he came up the slip, and when I gave the signal 'All right,' he put on steam boldly and went over without trouble. He offered to stay there and take all the trains over, but was not allowed to do this.

After a big lift of the road, and a quantity of fresh faggots and sand had been put under the track to pack it up, these materials lay, of course, very hollow; and as the heavy engine passed over, the road sank down a couple of feet under the wheels of the engine, much like a wave of the sea, running along in front of the wheels, but there was never the least hitch or accident. Of course, there were no Board of Trade regulations affecting railways in those days.

Messrs Oldham completed the works in July 1841, the accounts being adjusted before the end of September by liberal concessions on the part of the CGWUR, the contractors agreeing to accept the balance by instalments 'which best suited the convenience of the company'. All seemed well until the summer of 1842 when Messrs Oldham made a further demand, the CGWUR claiming they 'do not understand upon what principle accounts so settled and acquiesed in by all parties, can be successfully re-opened by the assignees of the Contractors'. The outcome of the dispute was that the CGWUR had to pay all legal costs despite the fact that Oldham's had only established a seventeenth part of their claim.

On 15 March 1842 an accident occurred on the Cirencester side of Kemble station. On the embankment, which was about 50 feet high at that point, was a pulley and ropes for the purpose of loading ballast wagons with gravel, these standing in a siding. The *Wilts & Gloucestershire Standard* reported: 'By the neglect of the policeman there, the swivel point which had been turned to let some trains to load, was neglected to be replaced and the twelve o'clock train ran in with a fearful crash upon the ballast wagon then loading which was literally smashed.' *Meteor*, a Sun class 2–2–2 built by R. & W. Hawthorn & Co., in November 1840, together with its tender, was forced down the embankment for 20 feet, the coupling between tender and luggage van holding and preventing a fall. The driver and fireman were fortunate to escape with only a bruising. Kemble was a ballast centre as Rowland Brotherhood who held the maintenance contract of the line, for nearly seven years ran ballast trains from Tetbury Road.

In December 1841 the CGWUR directors met their Great Western counterparts receiving a proposition to purchase the completed line — a suggestion which the CGWUR directors could not accept as they wished to sell the whole undertaking. In July 1842 they met again, the CGWUR directors pointing out that if the GWR did not complete the line, the Birmingham & Gloucester would take all traffic from Cheltenham, Gloucester and South Wales via the London & Birmingham and the Great Western would make no profit from it. Meanwhile a CGWUR Act, 5 & 6 Vic c 28 of 13 May 1842 stated that in view of the fact that the £750,000 and borrowing powers of £250,000 were inadequate, it would be lawful for the directors to 'create new shares of such nominal Value as the Directors think fit . . . any further Sum of Money not exceeding in the Whole Sum of Seven hundred and fifty thousand pounds', it being lawful for the Great Western and Bristol & Gloucester to guarantee interest of the new shares. The company was given powers to sell to the GWR, Bristol & Gloucester, or Birmingham & Gloucester railways.

A special meeting of the CGWUR was held on 10 January 1843 for the purpose of considering the propriety of entering into an arrangement with the GWR, the Heads of Agreement listing:

1. The Cheltenham Company shall complete the line Kemble to Gloucester and from the Birmingham & Gloucester Company's station at Cheltenham to the CGWUR terminus.

2. The Great Western will defray the interest of £900,000 required to be raised for completion. The lease of the whole line to be £60,000. The section from Stonehouse to Gloucester to be completed by 1 March 1844, and Kemble to Stonehouse and Gloucester to Cheltenham by 21 June 1845.

A special general meeting of CGWUR shareholders was held on 25 August to approve a contract dated 8 June between their company and the GWR whereby the latter would pay shareholders 3,000 half shares of £50 each and £80,000 in cash to defray existing CGWUR debts. The actual transfer took place on 1 July, the GWR acquiring for £230,000, £600,000 worth of works. The final CGWUR account for December 1846 showed that shareholders received one GWR half share worth about £80 together with 17s 6d cash for every two CGWUR shares on each of which they had paid £83. Of the original 7,500 shares the GWR held 392, others 5,693, the balance of 1,415 having been forfeited for non-payment of calls. The amalgamation of the two companies was sanctioned by the Great Western Act 7 Vic c 3 of 1844. The last meeting of the CGWUR was held on 23 September 1843.

Kemble to Gloucester

The standard gauge Bristol & Gloucester Railway which received its Act of Parliament 2 & 3 Vic c 56 on 1 July 1839, negotiated with the CGWUR to use the CGWUR rails between Standish and Gloucester. In January 1840 the CGWUR was invited to take over the Birmingham & Gloucester and Bristol & Gloucester railways, but declined the offer, being in serious financial difficulties itself through arrears of calls on shares. At a meeting with the CGWUR on 17 November 1840 it was agreed that a third rail would be laid and maintained between Standish and Gloucester at the expense of the Bristol & Gloucester and remain BGR property. The BGR asking for a firm date for completion of the line, received a vague reply, the CGWUR merely saying that it would be the last section to be finished. As this was an unsatisfactory state of affairs, the CGWUR Act 5 & 6 Vic c 28 of 13 May 1842 sanctioned the BGR constructing the line from Standish to Gloucester, with optional repurchase powers being given to the CGWUR, though in the event the GWR took over the CGWUR and completed it.

Although contracts were let in 1837 for making the line from Cheltenham to Gloucester together with the preliminary shafts at Sapperton Tunnel, work does not seem to have started in earnest until 1839 when five of the permanent shafts were completed. In 1841 four additional shafts were sunk to facilitate cutting the tunnel. On 28 November the tender of Thomas Baker, a well sinker, Cirencester, was accepted for Sapperton Tunnel shafts Nos 1 and 2, and that of William Ritson of Rugby and Thomas Fowler for Nos 3 to 6. Richard Boxall of Grantham, a former pupil of the architect Augustus Pugin, was appointed resident engineer. On 29 December 1840 the directors discussed tenders for cutting the heading and that of Thomas W. & J. Fowler was accepted. Brunel's report of 3 February 1841 said that completion of the works from Kemble to Gloucester, excluding purchase of land, would cost £700,000 to £750,000. On 21 October the directors once again found occasion to criticise Brunel and resolved that he be required to reconsider his valuation of the locomotive *Vesta* which broke down when first tried and notwithstanding the expenditure of £470 in repairs by the CGWUR was 'perfectly useless'.

The line was let in four contracts and work began in August 1843, the first contract being opened on 8 July 1844 as part of the Bristol & Gloucester Railway. The second contract from Stonehouse up the Stroud Valley to Sapperton Tunnel was about two-thirds finished and ballasted by the summer of 1844, while the third contract, the tunnel itself, 650 yards of the 2,227 yards, remained unfinished, but workmen were busy night and day. Jonathan Willans Nowell had won this contract on the recommendation of Brunel because he had shown so much competence at Wickwar Tunnel on the Bristol & Gloucester line. The contract signed on 2 June 1843 showed a change from the 1838 Act. Sapperton Tunnel was to be made in two sharply graded sections with an open cutting at summit level between them. The original drawings show the tunnel on a gradient of 1 in 330, while as cut it was actually on a gradient of 1 in 90 — the formation being at a higher level than that originally proposed. By the summer of 1844 from Sapperton Tunnel to Kemble the line was ready to receive the permanent way.

On 3 July 1844 the proprietors of the Thames & Severn Canal wrote prohibiting further works of the CGWUR being carried out across its property as a considerable leakage of Bourne Pond above Brimscombe had been experienced as a result of the imperfect state of the masonry laid by the railway.

Several navvies suffered in building the line. Between 7 and 8 a.m. on 15 September 1844 George Freeman, aged 26, and Henry Stokes, (alias Smith), aged 33, were working about ten feet below 'an immense mass of stone two or three tons in weight' and beneath this Stokes was boring a hole to insert powder for blasting. Freeman was busy loading a wagon. Suddenly, without warning, the rock collapsed on Stokes' head and crushed Freeman killing him instantly. Both were immediately extricated. Stokes gave two gasps and died. Freeman was a local man from Bisley while Stokes came from Warwickshire. Their lives were needlessly lost as the rock could have been more easily removed with a pickaxe than by blasting. Two other men injured by the fall were only off work for a day. Four days later, as Edward Harratt was working in a stooping position with his back to the base of a deep cutting between Gloucester and Stonehouse, three tons of material slipped on him. Dug out dreadfully bruised, he was carried to his lodgings where he died two hours later. On 4 October 1843 George Dratsy was in Sapperton Tunnel cleaning a hole in which gunpowder had been placed when it exploded causing him to lose an eye.

An accident which could have had fatal consequences occurred near Standish Junction on 22 January 1845. The CGWUR works there were nearing completion and the contractors were removing stone for their work near Standish bridge and transporting it there on Bristol & Gloucester rails in between trains. A CGWUR policeman was assigned to the beat to see that all was safe. He locked the points to prevent the stone wagons entering the BGR lines. One BGR train passed safely and the constable warned James Moody, the ganger in charge of the contractor's wagons, not to move as it was nearly time for the second BGR train. The officer then moved on his beat.

Disregarding the instruction he had received, a few minutes later Moody unlocked the points and took wagons on to the BGR line. Moody saw a BGR train approaching and to ensure their safety, uncoupled the horses. Despite the BGR driver's attempts to stop, the BGR train struck the wagons. The BGR driver jumped off before the impact and was injured. Moody was taken before magistrates and committed for trial.

The Rev. F. R. Neve, Rector of Poole Keynes near Kemble, wrote the CGWUR a letter dated 12 November 1836 regarding the possible bad behaviour of workmen. He had been put on his guard by hearing poor reports of conduct of navvies on the London & Birmingham Railway. Farmers being forced to keep watch over their property on Saturday nights when the navvies were paid, the neighbourhood being 'filled once a fortnight with the riots of intoxicated parties, fightings, depredations and all sorts of violence'. The Rev. Neve suggested that the men be paid weekly and on a day other than Saturday, 'The reason usually given for preferring a Saturday or Sunday for paying the men is that the Contractors had rather that Sunday should be wasted in drunkenness than any other day'. In the event, to obviate any trouble, Henry Norris, inspector of brickwork, and two of Messrs Oldham's head workmen were sworn in as special constables. In December 1840 it is recorded that five special constables cost a total of £8 15s 0d a fortnight, the wages being fixed by the magistrates.

The directors of the Great Western pressed forward to finish the line from Kemble to Gloucester soon after they had taken over the CGWUR, as powers to buy back the moiety of the Gloucester to Cheltenham section from the Birmingham & Gloucester Company depended on the Swindon to Gloucester length being completed by 21 June 1845. Furthermore, they had agreed to have the portion from Standish to Gloucester ready for use by the Bristol & Gloucester by April 1844. By 1845 the tunnel and all principal works were complete and the permanent way was being laid.

Early in May 1845 the line was inspected by General Pasley accompanied by resident engineers R. P. Brereton and C. Richardson, it being opened for passengers only on Whit Monday 12 May 1845. The GWR announced:

The Directors regret that they have been precluded by the unexpected stoppage of their works at Gloucester on the land purchased for the station, from affording facility for other traffic, and even providing convenient accommodation for passengers for a short time, until they shall have been able to make satisfactory arrangements with the Birmingham & Gloucester Railway Company, or shall have acquired legal possession of their rights. The Great Western Line to Cheltenham also will then be completed with the least practicable delay.

The Birmingham & Gloucester withheld the use of Gloucester station for accommodating Great Western traffic in retaliation for alleged 'spiteful acts'. This dog-in-the-manger attitude was hardly unexpected as the GWR had prevented the Midland Railway, the new owner of the Birmingham to Bristol line, from laying standard gauge between Gloucester and Standish, while another bone of contention was over a payment and the fact that the GWR had set labourers to work on the Birmingham & Gloucester line between Gloucester and Cheltenham without giving the notice to which they were entitled. Public inconvenience was kept to a minimum by a heads of agreement:

May 9th — It is agreed that any question of account relative to the works between Gloucester and Cheltenham shall be settled forthwith by Mr Brunel and Mr R. Stephenson, with power to appoint an umpire in case of need.

May 10th — The Great Western Company desire to work their traffic into the Gloucester station, uninterruptedly, or to use or build upon the vacant land, for their accommodation. The Bristol and Gloucester and the Birmingham and Gloucester Companies object that such working or use might interfere with certain of their existing rights. With the view of obviating any possible inconvenience to the public, it is agreed that the Great Western Railway Company shall work their traffic into the Gloucester station, and use the vacant land until the question shall be determined by law, and with the distinct understanding that such working and use shall in no way prejudice the existing rights or positions of any of the parties, under their respective Acts of Parliament, or otherwise. In case the Great Western Railway Company shall place any buildings on the ground, and it shall afterwards be determined that they have not a right to the land, they shall be at liberty to remove them without making any claim upon the Birmingham and Gloucester Company for their value or cost. The above arrangement is not to extend to such part of the station as is now used by the Birmingham and Gloucester Company.

The GWR worked into a platform added to the north side of the Birmingham & Gloucester terminus and used by Bristol & Gloucester trains since the previous July.

The *Gloucester Journal* of 17 May 1845 reported:

On Monday, the Great Western line was opened throughout from London to Gloucester, since which time several trains have continued to run daily between this city and the metropolis. By this route Gloucester is 114 miles from London, or within four hours and a half distance reckoned by time. This is by the ordinary trains; but there is an express train to and fro each day which performs the distance in five minutes under three hours. On Monday last, this train accomplished the 114 miles in two hours and forty minutes. By this train, a person may leave London fifteen minutes before ten in the morning, arrive in Gloucester at twenty minutes before one, transact any business he may have to do in the next fifty minutes and be back in London by the return express train, by half past four the same afternoon; altogether only six hours and forty five minutes. The newly opened portion of the line passes through a most beautifully picturesque country, opening to travellers some of the choicest scenery of Gloucestershire.

W. Higgs, an excursion promoter, organised two trips from Gloucester to London for a three to four day stay. It was not too successful. That run on Whit Monday 12 May had 18 passengers and that of the 13 only 16, the fare of £1 1s 0d second class and £1 11s 0d first class being thought too high. Brimscombe and Stonehouse stations opened on 1 June 1845, Gloucester and Stroud opening to goods on 15 September 1845.

Following the partial opening of the South Wales Railway on 19 June 1850, the CGWUR became part of the main route to South Wales. In 1844 the GWR had revived the proposition of building the South Wales & South of Ireland Railway from Stonehouse across the Severn between Fretherne and Awre by a bridge 2,000 feet in length. The Severn Navigation Commissioners accepted the proposal, but the Admiralty vetoed the bridge, thereby putting a stop to the scheme. The reason is difficult to understand as most shipping used the Gloucester & Berkeley Ship Canal.

The Great Exhibition of 1851 encouraged rail travel and one female from Bath had good reason to remember her trip. The *Bath & Cheltenham Gazette* of 6 August 1851 recorded:

On Monday fortnight [23 July] a servant girl from Bath decided to see the wonders of the Great Exhibition. For reasons of economy, she selected the Parliamentary train, but she missed it. Nothing daunted, with a quarter's wages in her pocket, and something more, she preferred the next train to the next day, and soon she found herself passing the engine which was to have conveyed her to London, and this in some degree satisfied her for the extra outlay, forgetting that her altered plans in Bath would also operate at the London terminus. Here she failed to meet the friends who were to conduct her safely to her destination and in her dilemma sought refuge in a cab, with the request to the driver to take her to a certain street in Kensington; but, after numerous fruitless inquiries, Kennington was found to be the desired haven, which, after much perplexity, was reached at the cost of a six shilling cab fare.

Happy in meeting her friends, the young woman found no further annoyance till she went to the Crystal Palace, when her gratification was alloyed by a tremendous shower on leaving the building, which rendered her Exhibition bonnet and dress useless for the future.

The mishap which attended her at starting, appeared to follow her, for on her return, wishing to call on a relative in Gloucestershire, she inquired for the Railway which would take her to Stroud, perhaps without designating the county. She was referred to the London Bridge terminus and having purchased her ticket, a pleasant ride followed; but the sight of the sea gave her misgivings that she was wrong, and finding her journey at an end, asked the guard if that was Stroud, in Gloucestershire, when to her great dismay, she found herself at Strood in Kent.

Here, to the credit of the Railway authorities, no advantage was taken of the error, and being satisfied of the truth of the servant's statement, they returned the fare and sent her back to London, and the girl sustained no other inconvenience other than a return to Kennington. She was more careful in her next exploit, and on Monday evening reached home a little the worse for her numerous calamities, but with the full conviction that she never wished to see London again.

The Gauge Question

On 30 January 1845 the Midland Railway agreed to lease the line from Birmingham to Bristol, this throwing a spotlight on the break of gauge at Gloucester as it was very much in its interests to do so. Daniel Gooch, the GWR's locomotive, carriage and wagon superintendent, had designed methods for transferring goods between the two gauges, including that of having wheels sliding on their axles and standard gauge wagons being carried on broad gauge transporter wagons. However, neither of these ideas was put into practice.

Queen Victoria herself experienced the break of gauge at first hand when she visited Gloucester on 19 September 1849. Cholera was raging in London and it was thought

Swindon Junction, view west in mixed gauge days: to Bristol left, Gloucester right. Author's collection

Swindon Junction view east in mixed gauge days: lines on the lower left are from Gloucester. The passenger station is in the centre distance. Author's collection

safer that the Royal Family travelled from Balmoral to Osborne via Gloucester. The floor of the MR station where she arrived was covered with a scarlet cloth, a richer carpet being laid where the royal party crossed the platform. The appearance of the somewhat unsightly columns supporting the roof was enhanced by laurel and flowers. The *Gloucester Journal* reporter commented with admiration 'on the tasteful work of Mr J. C. Wheeler, of this City which formed a highly pictorial background for the rich dresses of the military and the flashing of swords and bayonets'. By means of the newly invented electric telegraph, information was received by the thousands waiting at Gloucester that the royal train had passed Cheltenham. 'The masses began to stir and hum with expectation, till amid the clashing of arms, the crashing of music and the loud cheers of the loyal multitude the train glided alongside the platform.'

Many railway officials were presented to her Majesty and all went well until the corporation and clergy came forward with their addresses.

Upon which the crowd behind them followed . . . and in their eagerness forced the Corporation and Clergy upon the Royal Carriage, oversetting the flower pots and interrupting the duties of the royal servants. However, the exertions of the mayor held the crowd back and her Majesty graciously presented herself at each side of the carriage . . . The royal children were especial objects of attraction, and formed an interesting group of young life, plainly yet elegantly dressed, while their cheeks bloomed with the roseate hues of health.

The Prince of Wales, then seven years old, 'wore a turn-down collar, encircled with a black ribbon tied in a sailor's love-knot; he is a fine, intelligent-looking boy'. The GWR engine *Warlock* of the Iron Duke class took the Queen to Swindon in 47 minutes and like many of her subjects, she used the station's catering facilities, graciously allowing it to be called the 'Queen's Royal Hotel'.

The break of gauge caused trouble and expense so a Royal Commission was appointed to look into the gauge question on 11 July 1845, evidence beginning on 6 August. When the Parliamentary Gauge Committee visited Gloucester to assess the situation for themselves, J. D. Payne, goods manager of the standard gauge Birmingham & Gloucester, craftily arranged for two trains which had been already dealt with to be unloaded to add to the work and confusion, so that the chaos the break of gauge caused would be the more impressive. G. P. Neale wrote in *Railway Reminiscences*:

When the members came to the scene, they were appalled by the clamour arising from the well-arranged confusion of shouting out addresses of consignments, the chucking of packages across from truck to truck, the enquiries for missing articles, the loading, unloading and reloading, which his clever device had brought into operation.

The utter confusion caused by the transhipment of luggage between gauges at Gloucester, 1846. Even the dog appears concerned. Courtesy: *Illustrated London News*

A further scene at Gloucester during the transfer of goods from one gauge to the other. The lady is experiencing great difficulty with her basket of ceramic ware. Courtesy: *Illustrated London News*

Because there were over 20 places where the break of gauge occurred, not only between the GWR and adjacent railways, but even between different sections of the GWR itself, the GWR directors decided to start converting their lines to the standard gauge. Ironically it was the survivor of the four broad gauge champions who was required to make the first official public reference to the question, when on 2 March 1866 Daniel Gooch, chairman and former Locomotive Superintendent, informed shareholders:

There is no doubt it has become necessary for us to look the matter of the narrow [ie standard] gauge fairly in the face. We have had within the past few days a memorial signed by nearly every firm of any standing in South Wales wishing that the narrow gauge might be carried out in their district. It is also pressing upon us in many other districts, and it will be necessary for us now to consider how this matter should be dealt with. That it will be a costly question there can be no doubt. We cannot look at it without seeing that it involves a large expenditure of money. How best to meet and deal with that expenditure is a question the Directors will have to solve, and that probably before we meet you again.

The South Wales line from Neyland to Grange Court was the first main line to be dealt with, the work being undertaken between 30 April and 12 May 1872. Conversion of the track from Gloucester to Swindon followed next, engineers taking possession of the Up line on Thursday 23 May, all traffic working in both directions over the Down line. To avoid head-on collisions between crossing stations, each section (Gloucester – Stroud; Stroud – Kemble; Kemble – Swindon) was worked by one pilot engine in the charge of a pilotman wearing a special badge on his arm. Much of the track was on longitudinal sleepers and to narrow the gauge, each transom was required to have about 2 feet 3½ inches sawn off, and the longitudinal sleepers slewed over to the new width.

Preparations had been made: transoms were marked where they needed to be cut; all bolts and nuts had been oiled so that they could be turned easily and new pointwork was prepared. To avoid moving men and tools each morning and evening, the line was divided into sections of about four miles, each length being provided with a central depot equipped with tools, smiths' shop, cooking facilities and sleeping accommodation, though the latter was not provided in towns, but lodging money paid. Each section had a gang of about 20 men placed in the charge of two gangers, an inspector supervising the work of two gangs. Coal, straw for bedding and oatmeal for making drinks were provided by the company and three shillings paid to each man, plus overtime for all work in excess of nine hours.

Because of the problems which would have arisen if conversion took place before all the broad gauge rolling stock was removed, most broad gauge vehicles were sent to Swindon, just a few being retained to work the limited service over the single line. The last broad gauge train left Gloucester following the midnight mail on Sunday 26 May 1872. After the engineers had completed the standard gauge passing loops on the Down line, standard gauge pilot engines were sent to replace those on the broad gauge which were then withdrawn. All working was then transferred to the Up line which had been narrowed, the first standard gauge train being the Down mail on Sunday night. Ordinary double line working between Gloucester and Swindon was resumed on Wednesday 29 May.

Locomotives

The first broad gauge engines used on the line were 2–2–2s for passenger trains and 0–6–0s on goods, with a small tank engine working the Gloucester T line. Gooch's standard gauge 2–2–2s, Nos 69-76 built 1855-6 were transferred to Swindon in the late eighteen-seventies after being renewed by Armstrong and these frequently worked to Gloucester. Ahrons said that for their size they were about the best single driver express engines that ever ran. Remarkably fast runners they could beat the Queens, though the latter could handle a heavier train. They coped splendidly with the four miles of 1 in 60/70 to Sapperton Tunnel with its continuous series of S–curves adding to the friction, taking trains of up to 130 tons, though with loads above this a bank engine usually assisted.

Queen class 2–2–2 No. 1122 *Beaconsfield* and No. 1123 *Salisbury* were shedded at Gloucester from 1875-1887 working to London on alternate days with the 8.00 a.m. from Gloucester, (a boat express from New Milford), returning on the 5.45 p.m. Milford boat express, not reaching Gloucester until 8.37 p.m., making a long day for the footplate crew. As the GWR and Midland Railway ran parallel between Gloucester and Standish Junction, it was too much to expect drivers not to race. *Beaconsfield* and *Salisbury* pulling the Up train were often beaten by MR 0–4–4T Nos 1280 and 1281 working a light train from Gloucester to Lydney via the Severn Bridge. Great Western men claimed that the Midland had the advantage, as the latter ran on a transverse sleeper road and not longitudinal baulks which were dead, drivers asserting that engines were 'two coaches better' over transverse sleepers. Ahrons also recalled that although GWR 2–4–0 No. 2201 took an Up mail over the 12 miles from Gloucester to Stroud in 14 minutes, it was badly beaten by Kirtley 800 class 2–4–0 No. 816. An early rule book issued by the Locomotive Department stated 'Great Western engines between Swindon and Cheltenham are distinguished from the Midland engines during the day, by having two white diamonds painted on the front buffer beam; and after dark by an additional white light under the normal one.' Bearing in mind the distinctive characteristics of GWR engines of the period, the need for this regulation during daytime is not apparent. In 1887 *Beaconsfield* and *Salisbury* were transferred to Swindon and replaced by Nos 73–76.

On one occasion, with the slow Up Sunday afternoon train during a severe snowstorm, the single driving wheel No. 118 *Prince Christian* started from Brimscombe without a bank engine and stuck fast at Frampton Crossing until an urgent telegraph brought the missing engine post haste. A bank engine at the rear was not, however, an unmixed blessing, especially on coal trains, although with these it was an absolute necessity. When coming over the summit at the eastern end of Sapperton Tunnel the train engine had necessarily to shut off steam to prevent the wagon couplings snatching. Frequently the banker would keep on pounding away and bump the coal wagons against the tender of the train engine in such a forcible manner that the latter would be suddenly propelled forward. On one of these occasions the fireman was tumbled over backwards on to the tender with an avalanche of Welsh coal on top, from which the driver had to excavate him.

When the Barnum class came out in 1889 these most successful Dean 2–4–0s set to work and were a great improvement on the 2–2–2s, climbing from Brimscombe to Sapperton. Two unusual 2–4–0s working on the Gloucester to Swindon road were Nos 7 and 8, Dean's essays into compounding. No. 7 worked for two years covering 7,546 miles, its greatest defect being the inaccessibility of the inside motion. Another fault was its propensity for the coupling rod pins to strike sparks from the coping stones of one or two platforms. Other 2–4–0s were the 2201 class, one of which worked a marathon 262 miles turn from Swindon to Neath and back. The crew booked on at 6.50 a.m., left Swindon at 7.50, made 32 stops en route to Neath, had two hours rest and started on the return journey with another 32 stops, arriving Swindon 8.05 p.m. and booking off at 9.00 p.m.

Great Western goods engines were used on a wide variety of duties and not confined to shunting or goods trains, finding regular employment on passenger trains and in some cases on what amounted to main line semi-express working. One such engine left Swindon at 4.48 p.m. as pilot on the heavy Hereford, Cheltenham and Swansea express, coming off at Stroud where, after half an hour's wait it picked up a long empty wagon train for Aberdare which had left Swindon earlier in the afternoon. This was duly deposited in Gloucester sidings at about 7.00 p.m. The next move saw the goods engine on a fast passenger, the 9.15 p.m. from Gloucester to Newport, a curious train which consisted of only two six-wheeled coaches and a goods brake van and stopped only at Lydney and Chepstow. From Newport the same goods brake van was taken to Tydu (Rogerstone) and about 2.00 a.m. a start was made on the return journey with a heavy coal train. This was a through run and when the crew reached Swindon at any time between 6.00 and 8.00 a.m. they felt they had done a good night's work. 0–6–0 saddle tank engines of the 1076 or Buffalo classes were used to haul trains over the 108 miles from Aberdare to Swindon.

Churchward Standard engines gradually appeared on the line, followed by those of Collett, the only locomotives not being allowed were those of the King class. Between 1917 and 1919 the Glasgow & South Western Railway lent seven 0–6–0s to the GWR, Nos 121A, 299A and 300A being shedded at Swindon and working over the line to Gloucester.

Loading Limit Swindon to Gloucester 1945

Maximum Load	Class of Locomotive
455 tons	Castle
420 tons	Star, Hall, Grange, Manor, Saint, 43XX, 31XX, 51XX, 61XX, 81XX, 56XX
364 tons	Bulldog, 44XX, 45XX, 57XX
336 tons	32XX, Duke, 2251, 0–6–2T 'B' Group
308 tons	0–6–0 and 0–6–0T, 0–6–2T 'A' Group

Working Instructions for Sapperton Bank, April 1894

At the southern end of the mouth of the second Sapperton Tunnel, trains must stop if necessary to pin down brakes. If pinned, a stop must be made at Brimscombe to take off the brakes. When necessary two goods or mineral trains may be coupled together to ascend the incline from Brimscombe to Sapperton and must not be uncoupled until they reach Tetbury Road or Kemble. Both train engines must be attached in front and a bank engine must assist in the rear. At Tetbury Road or Kemble the trains can be separated, or work as one to Swindon, the guards riding in their respective vans.
When Sapperton Tunnel signal box is closed (e.g. Sundays) the bank engine will work to Kemble instead of being taken off at the box. Up passenger trains assisted by Brimscombe bank engine must halt at Sapperton Tunnel up home signal and wait there for the bank engine to be disconnected and either placed on the up line siding, or crossed over to the down line, when the up home may be lowered. When an up passenger is assisted from Brimscombe to Sapperton the information must be sent from Brimscombe to Frampton Crossing and Sapperton Tunnel signal boxes on the single needle telegraph.

The 1925 Working Timetable Appendix stated that: 'When it is necessary to assist a Down Freight train from Kemble or Coates to Sapperton, the Bank Engine must be attached in front of the Train Engine and work through to Brimscombe in the same manner'. It had to assist as pilot because of the requirement to halt at the Frampton Stop Board, and a banker could not judge this stop if assisting at the rear. Such a banker would be supplied by Brimscombe shed on advice from Swindon.

The October 1960 Working Timetable Appendix regarding working from Stroud or Brimscombe to Sapperton Sidings stated:

When an Up Freight train required an assisting engine at Brimscombe, the train must be drawn over the Engine Shed points and when the train has been brought to a stand the Guard must signal to the Signalman that the train is clear of the points.
When an Up Freight train requires an assisting engine from Brimscombe during the time Sapperton Sidings Signal Box is switched out, the assisting engine must be coupled to the rear of the train at Brimscombe, and so work through to Kemble, but must not assist the train between Sapperton Sidings and Kemble.
Should an Up Freight train arrive at Brimscombe worked by two engines in front, (and a third engine is not required at the rear to assist up the Incline), the leading engine must be detached and assist at the rear from Brimscombe to Sapperton Sidings, where it must again be put in front if it is required to assist beyond Kemble.
When necessary an assisting engine may assist a Freight train at the rear from Stroud to Sapperton Sidings, providing the assisting engine is coupled to the train, the train to stop at Sapperton Sidings for the assisting engine to be detached.

An engine after assisting a Freight train from Brimscombe to Sapperton Sidings can run at the rear of the train to Kemble, providing it is coupled to the Van in the rear.

In the absence of the protective measures normally provided by the runaway catch points in the Up Line between Stroud and Sapperton Tunnel at 100 miles 2 chains, 98 miles 51 chains, 97 miles 52 chains, 96 miles 78½ chains and 96 miles 20 chains when during repairs or obstruction the points are clipped and padlocked for the purpose of single line working (Rules 189 to 208), it will be necessary for freight trains, other than fully fitted trains, to be assisted in the rear. In the case of passenger trains the Guard to ride in the rear brake van. These instructions will also apply when the Down line is being used for single line working and trains run over it in the wrong direction.

When a banker was coupled to a goods brake van, it was normal practice for the guard to lean out of his verandah and uncouple the locomotive between the two Sapperton Tunnels to avoid stopping the train. As the Neyland to Paddington Night Mail did not stop at Brimscombe, the banker went to Stroud to pilot the train engine. If a passenger train required assistance the banking engine had to be coupled in front. When it assisted working, an engine returning light to Brimscombe could be attached to a Down freight from Sapperton Sidings, the signalman pre-arranging the working and the signalman at Brimscombe East being advised when the train left Sapperton Sidings with the assisting engine attached. At 5.30 a.m. on Sunday the Brimscombe banker returned to the Gloucester depot, no assistance being provided until its return that evening.

When a banker, or two on a heavy train, was buffered up at the rear of a goods and ready to depart, the banker sounded 3–1–3 code on its whistle, the driver on the front engine responding with the same code and both drivers opened their respective regulators.

The first appearance of diesel traction was in April 1936 when GWR diesel railcar No. 15 ran a Monday to Friday service from Cheltenham to Marlborough over the Midland & South Western Junction Railway, returning via Kemble, though due to lack of support, this innovation was withdrawn in September when the winter timetable commenced. Although the AC Cars four-wheel railbuses, which started working the Tetbury and Cirencester branches in 1959, ran from Kemble to Swindon for fuelling and maintenance, they were not permitted to carry passengers through to Swindon being too light to operate track circuits reliably. The usual diesel-hydraulic and diesel-electric locomotive types associated with the Western Region appeared in the nineteen-sixties, together with DMUs, while in 1978 the line was given the honour of having the first refurbished DMUs to enter service in the West of England Division. HSTs started running over the line regularly in May 1983. These, operated by First Great Western still run today, while more local trains are operated by first Great Western 150 class DMUs, 158 class DMUs and 158 class DMUs from South West Trains borrowed to replace 150s away for refurbishment.

Steam Railmotors

Early in the twentieth century an interesting and far reaching innovation began in the Golden Valley between Stonehouse and Chalford. In May 1902 Thomas Nevins, the American tramway pioneer and instigator of electric tramways at Cheltenham, sought powers to construct light railways from Chalford to Stonehouse; and from Nailsworth to Stroud, Painswick, Gloucester and Cheltenham. Although the application was

Steam railmotor No. 1 at the Up platform, Stonehouse 1903. Michael Farr collection

Steam railmotor No. 2 at the Down platform, Stonehouse. The conductor/guard stands beside the fireman, while the driver stands proudly in the cab doorway. The oval GWR maker's plate is between the cylinders. Author's collection

Steam railmotor No. 1 at the Down platform, Stroud. The front windows have been modified so that a standing driver can see forward without stooping. Author's collection

Steam railmotor No. 1; notice the trellis gate. No. 1 moved to Aberdare in 1908. Author's collection

The interior of auto trailer No. 170 built in 1928, at Stonehouse 14 January 1929. Author's collection

Steam railmotor No. 11 at Stonehouse *c.* 1904. Author's collection

Interior of a steam railmotor. Straps are provided to assist standing passengers. The card is postmarked 8 April 1904. Author's collection

disallowed on grounds of competition with the GWR and MR, the syndicate applied to Parliament for authority to construct and work tramways on the routes disallowed by the Light Railway Commissioners. In view of the local feeling and existing facilities for local traffic, mill and factory workers having to use horse buses as existing stations were too far apart and trains too infrequent to tap this traffic, the GWR felt that powers might be given to authorise construction of the projected tramways. Because of the topography, inhabitants lived principally on the hillsides and as both the railway and proposed tramway kept to the valley floor, they were placed on almost equal terms as regards facility of access. A GWR report issued on 31 December 1902 said: 'In these circumstances the question arises whether the Great Western Company cannot by introducing a quick and efficient local service between Chalford and Stonehouse, make it commercially impracticable for a tramway to be constructed in the district to compete with the Railways'. The GWR was very fearful of road competition as not long previously, the opening of the Camborne & Redruth Tramway had reduced passengers carried by the GWR between these stations from 33,973 in 1901 to 7,859 in 1902.

In 1901 the GWR had carried 68,220 passengers between Chalford and Stroud bringing in receipts of £917 12s 6d and it was stated before the Light Railway Commissioners that buses carried eight passengers for each rail passenger, so something like 545,000 passengers were carried by bus. A GWR report of 20 April 1903 revealed that railway officials:

Whilst preserving an incognito . . . held conversations with various persons unconnected with the Company and have judiciously questioned a considerable number of railwaymen whilst walking over the whole length of the line from Chalford Station to Brimscombe, Stroud and Stonehouse. Throughout the Stroud Valley between Chalford and Stonehouse, a distance of seven miles, there is a succession of villages nearly all connected, adjacent to the railway, with a population of from 30,000 to 40,000 people: these are all prosperous looking places, showing the people have spare pence for travelling, and that view is borne out by the extensive road travel seen to-day. There are indications on both sides of the railway of building developments.

The population of this valley thrive upon cloth making, silk weaving, the manufacture of buttons, pins, walking and umbrella sticks, and wood turning. There are cloth mills and wood turning works employing 600 to 800 hands, and pin mills employing 300 hands, in the villages all through the valley.

The streams furnish water of qualities peculiar to the requirements of these industries, and at a dozen or more places the streams have been dammed, and supply power for the purposes of the mills and works, either in aid of, or substitution for, steam.

The local rail service at present consists of six trains in one direction and five in the other: i.e.

Down: Chalford to Stonehouse

a.m.	a.m.	p.m.	p.m.	p.m.	p.m.
8.43	9.55	2.19	5.41	7.57	9.10

Up: Stonehouse to Chalford

a.m.	noon	p.m.	p.m.	p.m.
9.13	12.0	3.36	7.03	8.21

Omnibuses run between Chalford and Stroud every hour and between Brimscombe and Stroud every half hour: there is a frequent service also between Stroud and Stonehouse. The services are supplemented on market days and Saturdays by additional vehicles. We saw on a Saturday evening, in the streets at Stroud, six omnibuses, (not carriers' carts), with a carrying capacity of twenty-five passengers each, loading at one time within sight of each other.

The shopping element encourages the tramway idea, but the residential element opposes it. The possibility of opposition from the residential element will be understood when it is stated that on all the projected tramway routes one sees quite an unwonted number of good class residences bordering on the line of route, and these are occupied by owners of the Mills and Works in the vicinity.

The number of trains it is possible to get over this part of the line is governed by the passage of bank engines returning light on the down line as far as Brimscombe after assisting trains up the Brimscombe bank. It is found that on one of the busiest days between 6 a.m. and 10 p.m., 49 trains and engines passed on the down line and 25 on the up line between Chalford and Brimscombe. The present occupation of the down line between those points is the measure of what additional trains can be put on.

But for the fact that the South Wales & Bristol Direct Railway had been opened on 1 July 1903, diverting trains from South Wales via Badminton instead of Gloucester, an intensive railmotor service could not have been introduced as there were insufficient paths between trains. The report proposed running an hourly service at first from 6.00 a.m. until 10.00 p.m., and if it met with success, increasing it to half hourly. The report pointed out that a car need not be shunted at the termini as it could start from the arrival platform. The level crossing halts would be manned from 8.00 a.m. to 8.00 p.m. and signals placed at danger while cars stop:

. . . if we cannot get rid of the obligation of using them for "protecting the stopping trains" but we strongly recommend that an effort be made to induce the Board of Trade to relieve the Company of this obligation, not only for these places in particular, but in view of future developments in the same direction in other districts.

The report proposed a charge of ½d a mile with a minimum fare of 1d. The proposed reduction in fares from Chalford to Stonehouse would reduce the income from existing traffic to £482, but it was anticipated that the deficit of £1,768 would be recouped by additional traffic. (The deficit was equal to 282,880 passengers at ½d each). The report pointed out an additional benefit which would be gained by the introduction of an intensified service: *It is well known that the Midland Company actively compete with the Company for the traffic of the District and by effectively catering for the local passenger traffic, the whole of the district would be educated to look more to the Great Western Railway for their railway facilities.*

In 1903 the LSWR and LBSCR Joint Committee built railmotor No. 2 — a coach and locomotive combined on the same underframe. This vehicle could be driven from either end, and was therefore ideal for working short shuttle services as it obviated the time and energy needed to run the engine round to the other end of the train at each terminus. The GWR sought permission to borrow it as they were in the process of building their own motors. On 7 May 1903 general manager Sir Joseph Wilkinson said: *The London & South Western have consented to lend the Motor Car from 6.0 p.m. on Saturday when it will be transferred to Kensington Addison Road, until 9.0 a.m. Monday, when they desire it to be returned at the same place.* The car was hauled from Nine Elms to Swindon on Saturday evening 9 May and from Swindon to Chalford on the morning of the 10th, Drummond's assistant, Sisterton, accompanying the vehicle.

The *Stroud Journal* of 15 May 1903 reported:

News of the proposed trial trip reached Stroud on Saturday, and all down the line groups of interested spectators had gathered to have a view of the new departure. The motor ran from Swindon, and the car was well-filled with passengers, including officials from Swindon works and most of the district traffic and permanent way inspectors. Contrary to expectations it did not arrive until nearly twelve o'clock, although a considerable number of people had assembled as early as ten o'clock, and waited with some impatience. It was understood, however, from intelligence which filtered down the line by means of passing goods trains, that the motor was stopping at several crossings, and this proved to have been the case. The engine was at the rear when it steamed into Stroud. A general stampede of people ensued from the "up" to the "down" line, but the car hardly stopped for a minute on its way to Stonehouse, where it returned later in the afternoon. The officials (including J. C. Inglis, general manager and G. J. Churchward, locomotive superintendent) partook of luncheon served in the waiting room at Stonehouse.

This LSWR vehicle was not suitable for the Stroud Valley, being designed for the mile-and-a-quarter long branch from Fratton to East Southsea where it eventually started work on 31 May 1903. Between Brimscombe and Chalford, with a load of 30 passengers speed did not exceed 8 mph on the gradient and 27 mph on the level. On the two seven-mile runs from Chalford to Stonehouse steam pressure dropped from 150 lb per square inch to 80 and 60 lb respectively. Uphill it fell to 100 and 80, even less being recorded between stopping places and the car had to wait to raise steam. Churchward witnessed the trials and took particulars of acceleration, running speeds and time occupied in stopping and was confident that the GWR car would be of ample power and steaming capacity for the work. Some supporters of the tramway scheme were interested spectators at Stroud.

The idea of the GWR having railmotors was first put forward by its general manager, Sir J. L. Wilkinson when he saw a paragraph in The *Globe* of 18 October 1901 regarding a self-propelled railcar being tried on the Northern Railway in France. He wrote for details as the chairman and some of the other directors were anxious that the GWR should be first in the British field. A frame was laid down at Swindon in January 1902 and a letter of 18 March 1902 from Dean, the GWR locomotive engineer, to Wilkinson read: *'Have the construction of a light locomotive for burning oil fuel well advanced and hope to have it ready for experimental running in three months.'* This 'light locomotive' was intended for railmotor working and shunting. On 29 May Dean wrote, *'Expect engine to be ready for experimental running in three weeks'*, but in the event he was unable to get the engine to work. On 11 October, Churchward, who had succeeded Dean, wrote to Wilkinson *'Preliminary designs for a combined carriage and motor have*

Official notice issued September 1903 giving details of the new steam railcar service between Chalford and Stonehouse.

been prepared and will go into it again and submit best design for Mr. Inglis' approval as to weight etc.' Wilkinson wrote to Churchward on 13 March 1903: *'It is now some 18 months since I begged your Department to try and help us, but no assistance has yet arrived.'* A design drawn by Collett was sent to Wilkinson on 21 April with the promise of plans for a petrol driven vehicle to be sent the following day, though this latter project fell by the wayside. On 29 April the directors authorised the construction of three motor cars — two for service and one spare.

Cost to GWR:		£	Annual Expenses	£
3 motor cars at £2,000 each		6,000	Interest on Capital	400
6 stopping places at £500 each		3,000	Car running — wages, fuel, water	1,400
Stabling for cars		1,000	Wages of 2 guards	150
			Maintenance of cars	300
	Total	£10,000	*Total*	£2,250

As late as 11 September 1903 the idea of having no fireman was in vogue, Inglis who had been appointed general manager on Wilkinson's death earlier in the year writing: *'If there is difficulty in getting the driver of the steam car to fire as well — so as to save a fireman — consider whether the driver should be required to get his steam* up before, starting with coal, and to keep up steam during his running, to turn on a petroleum (crude) spray over the fire. Maybe in this way one man could drive such a locomotive satisfactorily.'

The *Stroud Journal* of 16 October 1903 reported:

The new motor car service on the Great Western Railway between Chalford and Stonehouse Stations commenced on Monday, [12 October], and throughout the day the cars were well patronised, those in the morning and evening being crowded.

On Friday [9 October] a large number of press representatives and others, who were accompanied by Mr J. C. Inglis, general manager of the line, Mr C. Aldington, Mr W. Dawson (assistant superintendent), Mr G. J. Churchward (locomotive superintendent), Mr Marillier (carriage construction superintendent), and Mr Waister (locomotive and carriage running superintendent), made a trial trip on the car. Everything worked satisfactorily. The trip was made in good time with a full load, and the vehicle was well under control, even when stopping at crossings on the steep gradients.

The new cars, which were designed and built at Swindon Works under the direction of Mr G. J. Churchward, are handsome vehicles, 57 feet long, 8 feet 6¾ inches wide, and 8 feet 2 inches in height, inside measurement. The underframes, which are of steel, are carried on suspension hung bogies.

The total wheelbase of each of the vehicles is 45 feet 6 inches, that of the motor bogie being 8 feet and the carriage bogie 8 feet 6 inches. The cars can be driven from either end. Each car is divided into the following compartments:– Passenger, 39 feet long; motor, 12 feet 9 inches long, and vestibule 4 feet long. The structural framing is of Baltic and Canadian oak, the upper part of the outside being panelled with Honduras mahogany, and the lower part cased with narrow matchboarding. Electrical communication is provided for the convenience of the conductor and driver, and hand and vacuum brakes, which can be operated from either end of the vehicles, are fitted to each bogie.

In the passenger compartment all finishing work is in polished oak, and the roof is painted white, relieved with blue lining. This compartment will accommodate 52 passengers, 16 in cross-seats in the centre and 36 in longitudinal seats towards each end. The seats and seat backs are composed of woven wire covered with plaited rattan cane. The longitudinal seats are arranged in sets of three, each seating three passengers. The divisions of these seats, also the seat-ends of the cross-seats, are of polished oak, and support arm rests. There are eight large windows, fitted with spring blinds, at each side of the compartment, with two ventilator lights above each, which may be opened and closed by the passengers. Two brass rails, supported by pendants fixed to the roof, run from end to end of the compartment, to which are attached leather hand-loops for the assistance of passengers. The vestibule, which is at the end of the cars, is provided with steps, by means of which passengers can enter and alight at level crossings. Hinged flaps will cover the steps to allow passengers to enter or leave the cars at station platforms, and collapsible swing gates are fitted to prevent passengers leaving or entering the cars while in motion. Sliding doors of polished oak, with glass panels, allow of communication between the vestibule and passenger compartments. The cars are lighted by gas lamps, 14 candlepower each. The gas is stored in cylinders attached to the underframe. There are six duplex burners in the passenger compartment, one in the vestibule, and two in the motor compartment.

Steam for the engines is supplied by a vertical tubular boiler [fire-tubes], 4 feet 6 inches in diameter and 9 feet 6 inches in height, situated in a compartment at one end of the car. The engines are placed underneath the vehicle, and the cylinders drive on the trailing wheels of the bogie, which are coupled to the leading pair of wheels. The wheels are 3 feet 8 inches in diameter, and, with the boiler working at 180 lb pressure, the tractive force equals 8,483 lb. Water for the boiler is carried in a tank fixed under the car. The capacity is 450 gallons.

The public is already aware of the stations at which the cars will stop, and the time-tables are also published by the company. The cars will run at every hour from Chalford, and at the half-hour from Stonehouse, and the single journey will occupy about 23 minutes. There will be no service on Sundays. Tickets will be issued to passengers in the train itself on the tramway principle, and the second car will be held in reserve, which will be available whenever necessary.

During the week the service of cars has worked well, although for a short time on Tuesday there was a slight hindrance, which was easily remedied. On Monday 2,500 passengers were carried, and the traffic has been well-sustained.

Mr May, station-master [although in charge, he was not technically stationmaster], *at Chalford, who has charge of the working of the cars, furnishes us with the following figures. Number of persons travelling by the car: Monday, 2,500; Tuesday, 1,700; Wednesday, 1,200. The amount of money taken for the three days was respectively £20, £17, and £11. The management of the new scheme necessarily entails a great amount of extra work for Mr May, but he has carried out his new duties efficiently.*

On Saturday nearly 5,000 passengers were carried, the two cars running coupled together '. . . *and on each journey were crowded to excess. We understand that a great many people were unable to board the cars at some of the crossings*'. Return fares were: Stroud to Chalford 6d; Stroud to Stonehouse 4d. On Thursdays and Saturdays the motors ran to and from Gloucester dispensing with a special train at 11.05 p.m. Gloucester to Stroud and back. The railmotors worked with the locomotive end towards Chalford as did the auto trains of later years. Luggage was limited to light articles in the passengers' own charge, except those holding a through ticket to stations beyond Chalford and Stonehouse.

A unique feature of the Great Western scheme, not first adopted by the North Eastern Railway and the LSWR/LBSCR which were the first railmotor users, was that cars did not stop only at stations, but also at four level crossings, the object being to enable them to pick and drop passengers close to their homes in a similar way to an electric tramcar.

Colonel H. A. Yorke inspected the arrangements on behalf of the Board of Trade on 27 December. He said that although the Board of Trade had agreed to steps on the railmotors to obviate platforms at halts, the company had found it expedient to provide 100 foot long platforms looked after by gatekeepers, to accelerate the picking up and discharge of passengers.

Anomalies were found in the fare structure: Chalford to Ham Mill Crossing was 2d and Ham Mill to Stroud 1d making a total of 3d, yet the through fare from Chalford to Stroud was 4d compared with 3d on the bus. Similarly Brimscombe to Ham Mill was 1d and Ham Mill to Stroud 1d making a total of 2d the same as the bus, against a through rail fare Brimscombe to Stroud of 3d. Although taking a return ticket brought rail travel to the level of a return bus fare, passengers travelling to Stroud to join expresses would not be returning the same day and Inglis believed it possible that a proportion of these would travel by bus rather than pay an extra penny, people in the early nineteen-hundreds taking more effort to save small sums than those of today. Passengers from Chalford walking about half a mile to St Mary's Crossing could save 2d on a return ticket to either Stroud, Downsfield Crossing or Ebley Crossing. Inglis advocated opening halts at Bowbridge and Brimscombe Bridge as their absence enabled bus proprietors to maintain their services.

A memo from J. C. Inglis to T. H. Rendell read:

The present arrangement of issuing tickets on the Cars is somewhat troublesome in view of the fact that the Conductor, when issuing tickets, has to carry around the Car with him a small ticket case. Some relief might be afforded by making arrangements for the crossing keepers to issue tickets to those joining the Cars at stopping places, or Automatic Ticket Issuing Machines might be adopted. The latter course, however, might prove somewhat expensive, as the Sweetmeat Automatic Co. are asking a rent of £7. 10. 0 per annum for the machine in use at Lawrence Hill, or £100 to purchase outright. The machine at Lawrence Hill is only used for issuing one class of ticket, and the cost of obtaining machines to issue the different class of tickets employed on the Chalford and Stonehouse Service would probably be prohibitive. Negotiations have also been opened with another firm on the subject of automatic ticket issuing machines and it is possible more reasonable terms might be obtained from them. It might be desirable and convenient to issue books of tickets as is done on the Central London Railway.

If something could be done to improve the lighting of the approach to the Company's Chalford Station, greater advantage could be taken of the Motor Service than is at present the case.

To reach the Station every passenger has to cross a bridge over the Thames & Severn Canal, and at night, in the absence of any illumination, the road is extremely dark and dangerous, particularly so at the point where the road crosses the Canal. At this point the lamp in the Station Yard can be seen in the distance and anyone attempting to make anything like a bee line to the station, as would appear to be practicable in the day, runs the risk of falling over the bridge, the sides of which are low, and falling into the Canal. In fact I understand such a case did happen not so very long ago. This is of course really a matter to which the Local Authorities should attend, but at present the streets in the valley are not illuminated at night, and probably if the Parish Council were approached an arrangement might be come to under which the lamp could be provided, the Company contributing to the initial or annual cost.

There is also another question which in the future may become troublesome, and that is the encroachment on the Station accommodation. At the present time the Cars are illuminated by gas, and this involves the haulage to and from Chalford Station of a Gas tank, for the purpose of charging the cylinders under the Cars, and for which room has to be found in the Station Yard.

Now that it has been decided to provide trailers for use with the Cars, [the first trailers came into use 1904], a further encroachment will be made on the Station accommodation, and it is a question whether the Cars should not be lighted electrically in the same manner as the Central Corridor train, and thus save the expense of the haulage of the Gas tanks and the room occupied by them. Increased siding room could not be provided at Chalford except at great cost, and it is desirable that the space occupied by the Motor Cars and the accessories should be kept to a minimum.

The railmotors became so popular that in 1905 the GWR was forced to provide a bus service between Chalford and Stroud as the demand exceeded the railmotor's capacity, but it only lasted three months until further cars became available to augment the train service. Trailers were not the answer as the power unit was not strong enough to cope and difficulties were experienced keeping time. As a result the motors were converted into trailers by the engines being removed to give additional passenger space and were alternately pushed and pulled by auto tank engines of the 0–4–2T or 0–6–0PT variety. In the early days steam railmotors terminated at Stonehouse as the district onwards to Gloucester was relatively sparsely populated, so initially there was no need to run beyond, but in 1921 the service was extended from the Golden Valley to Gloucester. One fireman, wishing to show off, filled the firebox at Chalford and managed to reach Gloucester without adding any more fuel. The 0–4–2Ts were speedy and occasionally timed at nearly 80 mph between Stonehouse and Gloucester. The last railmotor in the Golden Valley stopped in July 1928.

Locomotive Sheds

Brimscombe

A stone-built single-road shed was situated at the southern end of the Up platform and was used latterly for stabling two bankers. It was enlarged *c.* 1872, probably soon after the gauge was narrowed. Opened in 1845 the engine there was allocated to Swindon until November 1856 when Brimscombe became a sub-shed of Gloucester. *Juno, Iago, Pluto* and *Bithon*, 0–6–0 saddle tanks of the Banking class were at work in the eighteen-fifties, an 0–6–0 of the Tyracmon class in July 1854, while *Romulus* a Gooch Standard Goods engine gave a hand in September 1856. Following the gauge conversion the 1016 class took on banking duties and later the 1076 or Buffalo class and members of the 2721 class appeared. 1902 saw a breakaway from 0–6–0 saddle tanks for banking when Aberdare class 2–6–0s worked until 1904, while in 1906 2–6–2Ts made their appearance, representatives of the 3100, 3150, 5101 or 6100 classes banking until the end of steam, when the shed was closed on 28 October 1963. Bankers were sent from Gloucester on a daily basis until 6 March 1965, but the need was reduced because of the introduction of diesels.

Water level in the Thames & Severn Canal above Beales Lock adjacent to the station, was required to be kept to the correct depth as it was used to supply water

5101 class 2–6–2T No. 4116 at Brimscombe shed awaiting a banking turn, 24 April 1962. A coal wagon is behind its bunker. Author

14XX class 0–4–2T No. 1458 working a Gloucester Central to Chalford train passes 4–6–0 *Fritwell Manor* waiting for a banking turn, 25 August 1964. Rev. Alan Newman

14XX class 0–4–2T No. 1458 passes Brimscombe shed 25 August 1964. As the shed roof is covered by a water tank, any smoke inside the shed is led up the timber chimney above the doorway. Rev. Alan Newman

to the shed. Even after the canal's abandonment in 1933 this length still continued to supply water to the railway. The original pump house built of timber stood on the south side of the line close to the canal, but in 1917 was replaced by a building on the north side. The pump in the latter was electric, being switched on when required by one of the drivers. Brimscombe engines carried the code GLO of the main shed, or 85B in BR days.

Chalford

The depot was a single-road corrugated structure opened in 1903 for housing railmotors. It was destroyed by fire, the *Stroud Journal* of 15 January 1916 recording:

About 2 o'clock on Sunday morning [9th January] an outbreak of fire was discovered at the GWR railmotor shed some distance up the line above the Chalford Station, and in a very short time the Stroud Volunteer Brigade (under Capt. Ford), the Stroud UDC Brigade (under Acting-Captain Cooke) and the Brimscombe Brigade (under Capt. Barrett) were upon the scene. PC MacKnight (Chalford) and PC Clifford (Stroud) were also in attendance. The nearest supply of water was the canal, which is fully three-quarters [sic] of a mile away, and the engines were only able to deal with the flames by linking up every available bit of hose. The whole of the shed and railmotor No. 48 was destroyed, but the firemen were able to take out a large motor trolley laden with cylinders of gas, and thus prevent a very serious explosion, the result of which would have been very destructive. The brigades ceased work about 8 o'clock on Sunday morning, and returned to their headquarters.

Although never rebuilt, the site continued to be used as a railmotor and later locomotive depot with pit facility until closure on 21 May 1951. A sub-shed to Gloucester it used the code GLO, or 85B in BR days.

Cirencester

The original broad gauge shed was replaced soon after gauge conversion in 1872 by a one-road timber shed. Although a sub-shed to Gloucester, the locomotive allocated was supplied by Swindon. The shed closed on 6 April 1964.

Gloucester

Gloucester opened as a small shed in May 1845 just east of the CGWUR terminus, but with the extension of the line to Cheltenham in October 1847 a depot opened there and engines ceased to be shedded at Gloucester. From February 1848 passenger engines for the area were stabled at Cheltenham, and goods and ballast engines at Gloucester. Following the increased locomotive allocation required by the South Wales Railway which commenced operating in 1852, a new four-road, brick-built shed was opened at Horton Road, Gloucester in 1854. A further six-road shed was added in 1872. On 31 December 1947 its allocation was 65 locomotives. By 1965 this had diminished to 35, including three locomotives which survived into preservation: No. 7029 *Clun Castle*; No. 6989 *Wightwick Hall* and No. 7808 *Cookham Manor*. Horton Road closed to steam in December 1965, all buildings, except the lifting shed, being demolished. The depot is still in use for stabling, signing on, fuelling and giving minor mechanical attention to diesel locomotives.

Swindon

The first shed at Swindon, situated near the junction of the Gloucester branch, officially opened on 1 January 1843, but was partially in use for some months

The GWR locomotive shed at Gloucester *c.* 1920, showing a fine signal gantry. Author's collection

A 4–6–0 Castle class locomotive with 'British Railways' on its tender, leaves Gloucester Central with a Gloucester to Paddington express, July 1948. Author's collection

A line-up of 14XX class 0–4–2T locomotives at Gloucester Horton Road 15 November 1964, awaiting disposal following the withdrawal of the Gloucester — Chalford and Berkeley Road — Sharpness auto services on 31 October 1964. Right to left the numbers are 1453,1458,1472 and 1420. The latter has been preserved. The coaling stage is below the water tank. Author's collection

Locomotives and two DMUs at Gloucester locomotive depot, 26 June 1986. Author

Swindon engine shed stands a short distance down the line toward Gloucester. This view *c*. 1893 shows a snow plough to the right. The main line is comprised of bridge rail on longitudinal sleepers. Author's collection

before this date. Constructed of timber it had stone corners and held a total of 48 locomotives and tenders on four roads. Following the abolition of broad gauge in 1892 the shed became part of the works. In February 1872 a nine-road standard gauge shed was built in brick on the up side of the Gloucester line. At a later date, a 21–bay roundhouse was added at the north end and in 1908 a roundhouse was built to the east with 27 bays. Its allocation on 31 December 1947 was 104 engines. The shed had the GWR code SDN which became 82C in BR days. The depot closed 2 November 1964. Today there is a one-road shed north-west of the station providing a fuelling point and emergency repair facility.

GWR Buses

On 9 January 1905 in lieu of building a light railway, the GWR inaugurated a road motor service from Stroud station to the Falcon Hotel, Painswick. Initially the vehicle was garaged at the Falcon until a corrugated iron shelter was erected in the station yard at Stroud. 1 March 1905 saw the service extended to Cainscross and on the same date, a double decker bus worked from Chalford to Stroud to ease overcrowding on the railmotor car service. With the provision of more railmotors, the Chalford service was withdrawn on 10th June together with the unremunerative Cainscross route. On 1 March 1905 the Painswick service was extended to Cheltenham, although after 9 July 1921 it terminated at Painswick.

During the General Strike in early May 1926, the restricted train service from Gloucester to Swindon was augmented by GWR buses which had been withdrawn from the Painswick service and diverted to running from Chalford to Gloucester, passengers obtaining tickets at the company's booking offices. On 30 May 1926 the GWR began a service from Stroud to Rodborough, and on 26 July Stroud to Kingscourt, while from 1 August the Painswick service was extended to Cranham on summer Sundays. On 20 June 1927 a new venture was started. A Maudsley charabanc operated a Land Cruise from Stroud, through the Forest of Dean, Wye Valley, across the Malvern Hills and through the Shakespeare Country to Oxford. By an agreement with the Western National dated 30 August 1929, Great Western bus services at Stroud were transferred to that company.

GWR 20 h.p. Milnes-Daimler bus AF 84 outside the Up platform, Stroud. It was first registered 18 May 1904. Author's collection

YH 3794, fleet No. 1222, a Maudslay chassis with a Buckinghamshire body at Stroud, 1 November 1927. It was first licensed 30 May 1927. Author's collection

Accidents

Mercifully accidents to trains on the Gloucester to Swindon line have been few. A mishap occurred to an excursion train carrying passengers to the Great Exhibition on 8 September 1851. It left Cheltenham at 11.30 a.m. with about 460 passengers in 12 coaches; at Gloucester 8 more carriages were attached and a further 3 at Stroud, the train then having a complement of nearly 1,200 passengers. At Brimscombe yet more passengers were squeezed in, while a pilot engine was attached at the front to assist up the gradient of 1 in 60 to and through Sapperton Tunnel. On emerging the other side, the train driver discovered to his horror that half his train was missing.

He blew his brake whistle to attract the attention of the guards, automatic brakes not being fitted at this period. '*After a brief consultation it was determined to start one of the engines along the other line to warn the mail train, which was known to be due, of the impending danger from the increasing impetus of the carriages down the incline — especially as it was known that only one guard was with them, whose attempts to check their progress might be ineffectual to prevent accident.*'

The pilot engine was detached to give this warning, but the driver of the mail train having fortunately perceived the carriages running down the incline towards him on the same line, immediately put his engine into reverse and cleverly managed to receive the descending coaches on his buffers with only a very slight shock. It was learned that some of the passengers, seeing the mail approaching and believing a collision inevitable, had jumped from the compartments. Apart from 'severe bruises' they were none the worse.

The mail train had proceeded forward with the runaway carriages to the Tetbury Road station where the remainder of the excursionists had arrived in safety, and greeted the arrival of their companions with rounds of cheering. Those who had been much too injured or frightened to proceed remained there, and the train continued on its journey.

It was found that the coupling had broken when the train was about three-quarters of the way through the tunnel, but the passengers in the 13 runaway coaches were not able to observe that they were proceeding backwards until they emerged from the portal by which they had entered. '*At this moment the up mail made its appearance on the same line of rail and added to the fearful consternation.*' The accident should not have occurred because in order to guard against such breakaways, in addition to the main coupling, there were two side chains. Unfortunately some careless person had omitted to hook on these safety devices. A subscription was started to reward Henry Wilkinson, driver of the mail, for his quick thinking. Eleven days later the *Gloucester Journal* reported:

We hear from the best sources that the amount is as yet comparatively — we may say disgracefully — small; many of the passengers even, whose lives or limbs have been saved, declining to contribute anything. This, as a public matter, ought to be generally responded to, for Wilkinson's judgment and coolness deserve rewarding with something more substantial than mere newspaper praise. We hear that thanksgiving services will be performed in several places of worship in this county on Sunday next, in consideration of the providential escape of the numerous passengers.

Despite the fact that early boilers were fitted with safety valves, boiler bursting was by no means uncommon. Between 10.00 and 11.00 a.m. on 7 February 1855 a large proportion of Gloucester inhabitants were startled by a loud explosion '*similar to the discharge of ordnance*' coming from the direction of the railway station. *Actæon*, a 2–2–2 of the Fire Fly class built 14 years previously, had arrived shortly before with the 6.00 a.m. from Paddington which it had headed from Swindon. The second coach being defective, it was decided to remove it before the train continued to South Wales. *Actæon* had shunted it to a siding and was within 15 yards of the platform when the boiler exploded, flinging parts of the engine in all directions. One piece of the boiler was blown through the wall of the adjacent workhouse hospital, while the damper rod weighing about 14 lb fell in Parker's Row, some 400 yards distant. It was very fortunate that no one was killed and only one man injured. He was John Cooke, a switchman about to speak to the driver when the explosion took place. The driver and fireman were lucky to escape. The militia were being drilled in

Fire Fly class 2–2–2 *Actæon* following a boiler explosion at Gloucester 7 February 1855. Author's collection

the New Market '*and the loudness of the report and the noise and confusion caused by the flying fragments caused a panic amongst the men. Several immediately threw down their muskets, while all rushed about bewildered from one place to another, and we believe it was some minutes before some recovered their proper senses.*' The train left only about 30 minutes later. *Actæon* was fitted with a new boiler and returned to service the following year.

Vandals are not a modern phenomenon. In April 1878 an award of £10 was offered for the apprehension of persons who placed a large stone on the track near Stroud on two successive Saturday nights just before the mail was due and almost causing the derailment of a goods train. Three youths appeared before the magistrates, but the case was dismissed through lack of evidence.

Permanent way men were always at risk and an instance of a fatal accident happened on 27 January 1877. Between Tuffley and Standish the Great Western and Midland lines ran parallel and it was near the mouth of Tuffley cutting that the accident took place. Four GWR gangers were employed packing the Down line to ensure a level track. About 11.00 a.m. Up and Down Midland trains passed, smoke and steam beating down on the lines and preventing the men observing a Great Western engine and brake van approaching on the Down line. Ganger John Manns was killed instantly, George Stone being seriously injured. The driver stopped and carried the body and the injured man to Gloucester. George Whitcombe, the solicitor of the deceased's widow, believed that the Great Western engine was racing the Midland express. James Batt, the GWR driver, said that when he arrived at Standish Junction the Midland train was about 300 yards ahead and kept this distance all the way to Tuffley Bank. As the coroner and jury refused an adjournment to allow production of signalmen's registers giving times the trains passed, George Whitcombe wrote a letter to the *Gloucester Journal* saying that '*It has often been stated that along this five mile run trains frequently race and I contend that the travelling public are entitled for their own protection to have these rumours cleared up*'.

About 5.00 p.m. on 13 April 1896 platelayers were at work in Sapperton Tunnel and when getting out of the path of a Down train, they failed to notice the noise and lights of one on the Up line, two being killed outright and another dying on the way to hospital.

The Great Blizzard of 1881 did not leave the line unscathed. On Monday 17 January a piece of iron roofing 50 yards in length was blown from the roof of Gloucester station, while a tree was pushed across the railway at Sapperton, bringing down the telegraph wires. On Tuesday evening the 1.50 p.m. ex-Paddington was snowed up near Tetbury Road and had to be drawn out of the drift by two engines. Instead of arriving at 6.07 p.m., it came in between 11.00 a.m. and noon on Wednesday. After that, no Down trains appeared all day and the London papers were not received until Thursday morning.

A serious derailment was narrowly avoided on 8 December 1888 at Bowbridge level crossing. A length of timber 18 feet by 2½ feet was being hauled across on a trolley when the 9.00 a.m. Paddington to Cardiff approached. The horse was unhooked and taken out of harm's way before the locomotive struck the timber and threw it aside. It was fortunate that the locomotive was only damaged and not pushed off the track.

In the early nineteen-fifties a driver felt a lurch as he passed through Sapperton Tunnel. The Brimscombe banker sent to investigate, discovered the trackbed had collapsed into a deep shaft of the original boring of the tunnel which had been planned to be cut at a lower level to reduce the gradient.

Early on 18 October 1961, No. 4945 *Milligan Hall* on arrival at Brimscombe with a Down goods was shunted across to the Up line in order to clear a path for a Down express passenger train to overtake. Before the Down freight could regain its correct road, an Up freight drawn by No. 6993 *Arthog Hall* passed three signals at danger and crashed head-on into No. 4945. Apart from serious front end damage to both locomotives, several wagons were destroyed. The nearby water column and a signal were demolished and the banking engine, standing close to the shed, was also damaged. The only casualties were one driver and a guard who were slightly injured. The line remained closed until the late afternoon of the 18th.

On 17 February 1969 the 17.30 Cheltenham to Swindon train, a three-car Cross-Country DMU containing 50 passengers, was derailed in the Sapperton Tunnel when its leading wheels struck a boulder weighing over a hundredweight which had been dislodged by frost and fallen down a ventilating shaft. After a delay of two hours passengers were transferred to a train brought from Swindon, while the 15.15 Paddington to Cheltenham had to be diverted via Yate.

Description of the Route

Swindon station (77 miles 24 chains from Paddington) opened on 14 July 1842. It consisted of two three-storey stone buildings 170 feet by 37 feet forming two island platforms of which the two inside roads were used by Bristol trains and the outer by those to Cirencester, the island design facilitating interchange. The buildings were constructed free of charge by Messrs J. & C. Rigby and leased back by the GWR for a penny a year, the railway company undertaking to make a refreshment stop for ten minutes, Rigby's more than recouped their investment by the profit they made on catering. The basements contained the kitchens and offices; the ground floor had the first and second class waiting rooms, while the upper floors were an hotel.

The buildings were linked by a covered footbridge used by passengers and hotel guests until a subway was built in 1870, after which the bridge was solely used by the hotel. Although a refreshment stop was admirable in early days, it proved frustrating when speed became important, the GWR being obliged to buy the lease for £100,000 on 1 October 1895, enabling it to abolish the stop. On 26 March 1898 a fire burnt

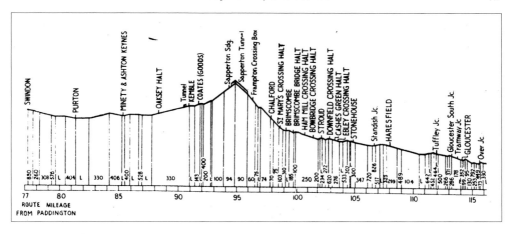

Gradient profile Swindon to Gloucester.

The east end of Swindon Junction *c.* 1900. In the bay platform a 4–4–0 heads an Up stopping train. A horse box stands at the Up main platform. Author's collection

Swindon Junction: view Up *c.* 1909. On the right is a water crane which can be used to supply locomotives on either track. Author's collection

A Down platform at Swindon *c.* 1909: doors for blanking corridor connections are on the right, with a line of milk churns, centre. Author's collection

Diesel-electric No. 45002 with a train of mixed coaching stock from Cardiff and Gloucester at Swindon 2 June 1982. Author

DMU set T305 works the 13.39 Swindon to Cheltenham 13 June 1988. It is painted in GWR livery. Author

Swindon Junction view Down *c.* 1890. Notice the mixed gauge tracks on the main line, but most of the stock is standard gauge. The train on the far right may have come from Gloucester. Author's collection

Swindon station after the fire 26 March 1898. Two milk vans stand on a centre road. The lady has a mountain of luggage. Author's collection

down the eastern half of the building on the Up platform and this was never rebuilt. The fire was caused through a wooden beam running across a chimney and aggravated by the fact that lead gas pipes ran down the flues. A new booking office was opened in 1873 and by 1880 three roads terminated near each end-face of the station building offering six extra platforms.

With the withdrawal of local trains in the Beeching era, fewer platforms were required, so the layout was rationalised by concentrating all traffic requiring a platform on the former Up island platform, this easing the efforts of passengers changing trains. The new layout was brought into use on 3 March 1968 coinciding with the introduction of an MAS (Multiple Aspect Signalling) signal box. The platforms were re-numbered, making two through platform roads, the northern No. 1 and the southern No. 3, with the bay platform at the west end being No. 2. Although the through platforms were signalled for reversible working, normally No. 1 was for Up trains, No. 3 for Down and No. 2 for the Gloucester DMU. One drawback with this scheme was that Down trains requiring a plaform had to cross the Up through road. To obviate this problem, Platform 4 on the Down side of the station opened on 2 June 2003.

West of the passenger station the Gloucester line curves sharply northwards with the former locomotive works to the west and the locomotive running shed and GWR brick works to the right. At 78 miles 20 chains the line becomes single, the other track being taken out of use on 28 July 1968 in the interests of economy.

The line crosses the trackbed of the former Midland & South Western Junction Railway which was closed to passengers 9 September 1961 and to goods 1 April 1964. Bremell Sidings (80 miles 24 chains) opened on 7 November 1943 and latterly, although fuel normally came in by pipe line, the rail alternative was available should a fault develop; also petrol could be temporarily pumped into rail tankers prior to cleaning the storage tanks. Due to bridge damage, the sidings were taken out of use 11 May 1987.

Purton station, (81 miles 36 chains) had its timber station building on the Up platform replaced about 1960 by a flat-roofed modern brick building, the timber waiting shelter remaining on the Down platform. The goods shed was constructed of brick and timber. To the north of the station a private siding off the up loop led to Hill's Brickworks, the siding agreement being terminated late in 1963 with the Up and Down refuge sidings being closed about the same time. The station shut to goods traffic on 1 July 1963 and to passengers on 2 November 1964.

Minety (85 miles 37 chains), renamed Minety & Ashton Keynes on 18 August 1905, had a typical Brunellan chalet-style wayside station building in brick with stone dressings. It had a small timber goods shed rather than a massive over-track building found at most of the other CGWUR stations. Minety closed to goods on 1 July 1963 and to passengers on 2 November 1964.

Oaksey Halt (88 miles 35 chains) opened on 18 February 1929, although the local inhabitants had petitioned for a halt 20 years previously. It had a corrugated iron shelter on each platform and dealt with milk as well as passengers. Although surrounded by fields it received a certain amount of use, for when the author visited it on 31 May 1962 seven bicycles were parked in the shelter. It closed on 2 November 1964.

Approaching Kemble Tunnel, the crumbling sides of the limestone cutting are held back by a breeze block wall. The tunnel, 415 yards in length and straight, has stone-faced portals and immediately to the north, the track doubles. From December 1995 it was no longer classified as a tunnel but an overbridge, yet remaining as a tunnel for inspection purposes. It was built by the cut and cover method. The two headings were misaligned by about a foot. The Down line was slewed from the tunnel wall to allow for the Locomotive Works water main to be laid. From November 1959 Kemble's Down distant was a colour light signal.

Bremell Sidings view north 1982. To secure the point tongue , a fishplate has been bolted against the side of the rail. John Mann

Bremell Sidings view Up 10 June 1989. The main line was singled 28 July 1968. Notice the grazing sheep. Author

Purton: an early view of one of Brunel's less grand structures. A Down broad gauge train approaches. The rails are on cross-sleepers, but broad gauge track was usually on longitudinal sleepers. The line was converted to standard gauge 25/26 May 1872, so this photograph pre-dates this. Author's collection

Purton, view Up *c.* 1910. Notice the white sighting-board behind the signal. Milk churns stand on the platform. Author's collection

Minety & Ashton Keynes view Down 31 May 1962. The goods sidings are quite extensive. Author

No. 7035 *Ogmore Castle* heads the 5-coach 11.45 a.m. Cheltenham to Paddington through Oaksey Halt, 31 May 1962. Author

Purton view Down in the early thirties. Beyond the timber station building is the goods shed. The station is neatly-kept. D. Thompson

The new station building in contemporary style at Purton, view Down 31 May 1962. Electric lighting has been installed. Author

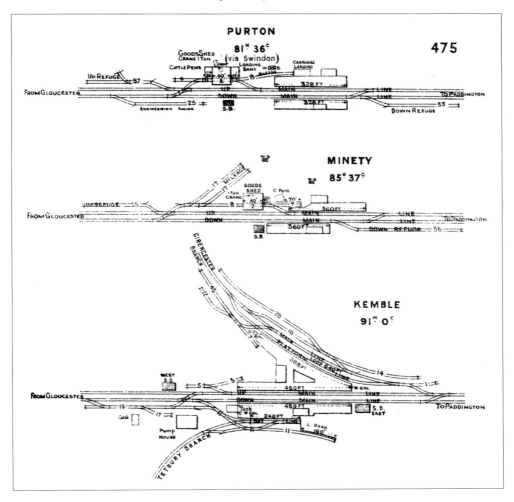

Station plans: Purton, Minety, Kemble. The figures on the plan indicate the wagon capacity of the sidings.

Kemble (90 miles 79 chains) was the junction of the branch to Cirencester and Tetbury and remains open today, enjoying commuter traffic to London. At first, Kemble merely had timber platforms for changing trains and possessed no road access, Squire Gordon not permitting a public station to be built on his land. The present station was the outcome of a Great Western director having a cold wait at the junction. Six acres of land were bought for £1,650 in 1881, an agreement being made with Miss Gordon that no intoxicating liquor would be sold on the premises and the only houses built would be for employees. Today's station with its mock Tudor design harking back to the railway style of 40 years before, was built in 1882 by Griffith Griffiths for £4,850, the tender being accepted on 9 February 1882.

The stone-built principal buildings are in the vee between the Up main and the Cirencester branch which still remains as a siding to the limit of what was the station yard. At least until the nineteen-sixties there was a bookstall on the platform. With the station's latest repaint the barley-stick-shaped cast iron supports carrying the platform canopy have capitals decorated with yellow daffodils and green leaves on a red

Kemble, view Down *c.* 1880. Notice the crossbar signal, water tower and on the left, the narrow platform. The branch to Cirencester curves right. Author's collection

Kemble, view Down *c.* 1905. The engine is taking on water. Cordon gas tank wagons for recharging coach lighting supplies, right. Kemble East signal box, left, closed in 1928. Author's collection

The station frontage, left, and Up platform at Kemble, 23 June 1979. A poster advertises 'Anywhere Return 50p'. Author

The footbridge at Kemble 30 July 1985. Author

Kemble station garden set between the Up Main (left) and the former Cirencester platform, 30 November 1985. Author

42XX class 2–8–0T No. 5206 on the Up line at Kemble having shunted a Down goods, 14 August 1962. Its condition shows that it is recently ex-Swindon Works. Author

A 94XX class 0–6–0PT enters Kemble with an Up stopping train comprising a corridor and non-corridor coach. Lens of Sutton

DMU set No. C821 works the 16.40 Gloucester to Swindon 30 November 1985. The blind merely displays 'Swindon' whereas in earlier days before the closure of Swindon Town station, 'Junction' would have been added. Author

The station staff at Kemble 1911. Author's collection

8750 class 0–6–0PT No. 8779 at Kemble with a mixed train to Cirencester, 6 September 1962. Each coach has a first class compartment. There are eight goods wagons. On the right is a cabin containing a 10-lever ground frame and the electric staff instrument for the branch. R. M. Casserley

8750 class 0–6–0PT No. 9772 arrives at Kemble with the 1.18 p.m. from Cirencester 21 July 1956. Author

ground, looking most attractive. A pleasant station garden is still maintained on the Up platform while hanging baskets of flowers are suspended above both platforms. Like the rest of the stations on the line, it became 'open' on 8 July 1984. At the north end of the Down platform was an important well. At first, water was raised by a horse-worked pump, but in 1872 Joseph Armstrong replaced it with one driven by steam and organised trains of rectangular water tanks on wagon frames in addition to using modified old tenders hauled by locomotives on a running-in turn. A second well, sunk *c.* 1890 was deepened in 1899.

In the early nineteen-hundreds the demand for water at the Works outstripped the supply by train, so in December 1903 a pumping station was opened between the fork of the Tetbury branch and the Down main. The floor level of the building was 13 feet 9 inches below rail level so as to reduce the water lift, and also allow the provision of gravity fed coal bunkers, which could be filled from coal wagons on the pump house siding. Although since 1935 the pumps have been electrically powered, until the end of steam traction, a Swindon Works trial engine went to Kemble on the first Thursday of every month in order to keep the steam standby pumps in working order. It is said that the opening of the GWR pumping station caused the spring at the nearby Thames Head, (the source of that river), to cease flowing regularly. Certainly by 1967 the water table had decreased to such an extent that a new bore had to be sunk and this was equipped with two new submersible two stage pumps, the old electric pumps and steam pumps being removed and the old wells plugged. As there was the danger of a burst main washing an embankment from under the track, a 'Burst Pipe' indicator was fitted in Kemble signal box and if it gave a warning, a light engine was sent to inspect the track. Latterly a warning was sounded at Swindon.

In March 1929 the East and West signal boxes were replaced by one central box and the opportunity was taken of extending the Up end the Down platform. Mr Baughn of Chalford bought both boxes for £6 os od and £9 os od respectively delivered free

The steam pumping engine at Kemble, November 1966. Lighting is by Tilley pressure lamp.
S. Apperley

The replacement pumping station 30 July 1985. Author

on rail to Chalford. He used them extending his house at Coppice Hill, the East box becoming his sitting room and the West box an outhouse and toilet. An interesting feature of Kemble is that due to the unusual road pattern, to travel by road from one platform to another involves a drive of over half a mile.

Tetbury Road, on the west side of the Fosse Way which formed the boundary of Squire Gordon's land, closed to passengers on 1 May 1882, the stone-built goods shed (91 miles 74 chains) remaining in use for goods traffic as this was not catered for at Kemble. To avoid confusion with Tetbury itself and avoiding parcels being consigned the wrong station, the goods depot was renamed Coates on 1 May 1908. It closed 1 July 1963. Here the line passes just to the west of the source of the River Thames. The line crosses the bed of the Thames & Severn Canal by a brick skew bridge. Sapperton Sidings signal box controlled sidings and loops used as a refuge by goods trains and banking engines which worked from Brimscombe. Although all sidings and loops were taken out of use on 8 September 1970, the Down loop was reconnected as an engineer's siding on 2 January 1973 but closed again in January 1981. As a safety measure in 1852 the inclines at both ends of Sapperton Tunnel were worked using the Cooke's electric telegraph and the absolute block system. There are two tunnels: the Short Tunnel 352 yards, then a short break in the summit cutting followed by the Long Tunnel 1,864 yards, on a falling gradient of 1 in 90.

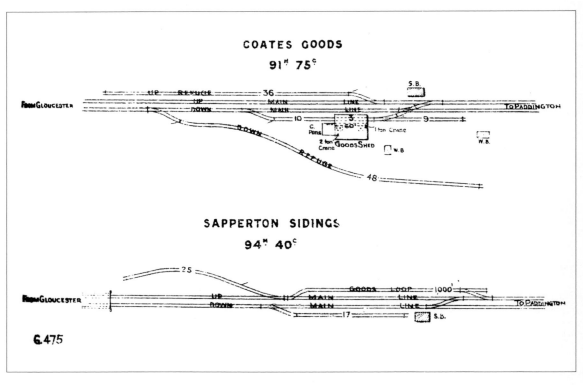

Station plans: Coates, Sapperton Sidings.

Right: An old rail forms a gatepost to the goods yard, Coates, 31 May 1962. Author

Below: DMU set C307 with the 13.05 Swindon to Worcester Foregate Street, near Coates, 1 November 1984. Author

Joint on welded track, Coates, 1 November 1984. Author

The CGWUR crosses the site of the Thames & Severn Canal, 11 May 1991. John Mann

4–6–0 No. 4915 *Condover Hall* passes Sapperton Sidings signal box with a Down express freight, 31 May 1962. Author

Sapperton Sidings and the east portal of the short Sapperton Tunnel; a former quarry on the right. 31 May 1962. Author

The Up Cheltenham Spa Express emerges from Sapperton Tunnel 12 April 1934. A cylinder is leaking steam seriously. L. E. Copeland

Hymek class diesel-hydraulic D7018 leaves Sapperton Tunnel with the 2.59 p.m. Cheltenham to Swindon 31 May 1962. D7018 has been preserved. Author

The Cheltenham Spa Express, the 10.45 Paddington to Great Malvern, at the east portal of Sapperton Tunnel, 8 May 1990. Author

A ventilating shaft of Sapperton Tunnel, 29 August 1985. The original stone wall has been raised first by bricks and then further by breeze blocks. Author

General Pasley's report to the Board of Trade gave the following description:

This tunnel has been cut through rock of the great and inferior oolites and fuller's earth formation, with shale and beds of shelly limestone. The rock being of an unsound quality with many wide and deep vertical and horizontal fissures, partly filled with clay or earth, it was deemed necessary to line it with masonry and brickwork throughout. The arch is a curve resembling an oblong segmental ellipse, of which the greatest span is 28 feet at the height of 7 feet above the rails, diminishing to 27 at that level. Part of it, 443 yards, has been formed with an inverted arch, of which the span is 27 feet at rail level, with a versed sine of 2½ feet. The side walls and invert are of masonry and generally 2 feet thick, while 20 feet in width of the upper part of the arch have been built with brickwork varying in thickness from 18 to 27 inches, that is from two or three bricks thick. Ten shafts were opened in making the tunnel, all of which have been blocked up except one only in the middle of the long portion.

In actual fact, at the present date two shafts are open for ventilation, spoil heaps marking the site of the remainder. Sapperton Tunnel closed for several weeks in the autumn of 2000 while a concrete raft was inserted as track was sinking into the canal tunnel.

King Edward VII travelled from Paddington to Gloucester and back on 23 June 1909 and the following regulations were required to be carried out regarding Sapperton Tunnel:

A permanent way man provided with hand signals and detonators must be stationed at each end of Kemble and Sapperton Short Tunnel at least an hour before the Royal Train passes in order to prevent any unauthorised person being on the railway in or near the tunnels and must remain until after the train has passed. The line is to be inspected through the tunnel after the previous train and before the Royal Train. No goods train is to run 30 minutes before, and passenger 25 minutes before the Royal Train. In Sapperton Long Tunnel a man is to be stationed every 220 yards through the tunnel. A man must be standing at the top of the tunnel at each of the two shafts (95 miles 8 chains and 95 miles 28 chains) at least an hour before and must remain until the Royal Train has passed, to prevent persons from approaching the shaft.

The line emerges from the west portal of the tunnel above the Golden Valley, this name being coined by Queen Victoria when she visited it one autumn. Just beyond the portal is a Stop Board at which descending freight trains were required to come to a stand and the requisite number of brakes pinned down and all traffic was restricted to a limit of 40 mph down the gradient with its reverse curves. The line crosses the 129-yard-long Frampton Viaduct with twelve 30 foot spans. Like the other viaducts on the line it was originally of wood and when this began to deteriorate, as it would have been difficult to replace without closing the line, it is believed that the timbering was encased in brick. A radar search revealed that this was not a folk tale and some timbers from the original viaduct had been left within as they could not be physically removed. By milepost 97 is an unusually steep occupation bridge designed by Charles Richardson carrying a footpath across the line on a gradient of 1 in 2.9, its purpose being to carry an inclined plane from Jackdaw Quarry to barges on the Thames & Severn Canal. This bridge has no less than three local names: Chalford residents call it Jackdaw Bridge; Frampton Mansell folk refer to it as Westley Bridge, while Oakridge people call it Skew Bridge. Chalford Viaduct, 220 yards is unusual in that being built on a steeply sloping ground it is one-sided. Its alternative name of Slip Viaduct comes from a landslip occurring some years before the railway was made.

Chalford station (98 miles 1 chain) opened on 2 August 1897. Built by T. H. Drew of Chalford, an embankment had to be made on the lower side to give support for the building. Originally the Up platform had a bay at its southern end, but this was fenced off by a sectional concrete extension when the platform was lengthened some time before the Second World War. The increase use of the station brought about by the introduction of steam railmotors caused the station's lighting to be changed from oil to coal gas for a cost of £93. Until closure one gas lamp managed to retain the station name in blue on an opal glass front. The GWR owned the land above the station, this including a spring in Cowcombe Wood and water from this was used at the station from its opening until closure. As the line at Chalford was on a gradient of 1 in 75, in the interests of safety, regulations stated that no passenger train or goods vehicle was allowed to be left on the main line without an engine being attached, while rolling stock in the Up siding was not to be uncoupled until secured by hand brake and also by sprags if the latter were thought to be necessary. The station closed to goods traffic on 12 August 1963 and to passengers 2 November 1964. Despite the suggestion from Inglis, auto cars remained gas lit until the end, gas tank wagons for replenishing the coaches being stored beyond Chalford signal box.

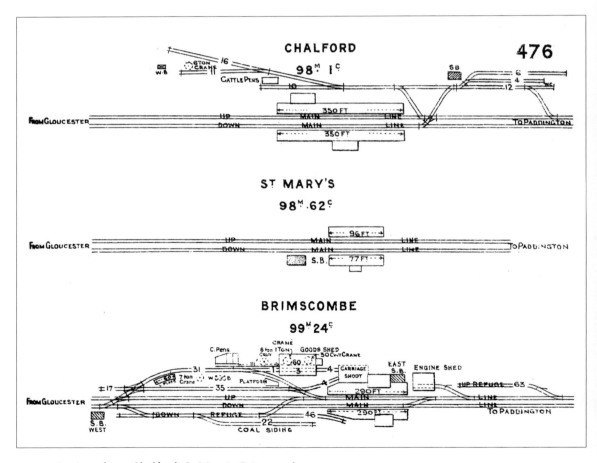

Station plans: Chalford, St Mary's, Brimscombe.

A o–6–oST heads an Up goods through Chalford *c.* 1903. Author's collection

Chalford *c.* 1910. Behind the Up platform is a cattle pen with the goods yard beyond beside the bank of the Thames & Severn Canal. The footbridge on the far left is of timber. Author's collection

Chalford *c.* 1910: the 4 coach set at the Up platform comprises a brake third, a third, luggage composite and a brake third. Beyond is a 70-foot steam railmotor trailer. Author's collection

Chalford *c.* 1910: Steam railmotor No. 32 right and a trailer left. No. 32 was built in December 1904 and in April 1920 it became trailer No. 130. Author's collection

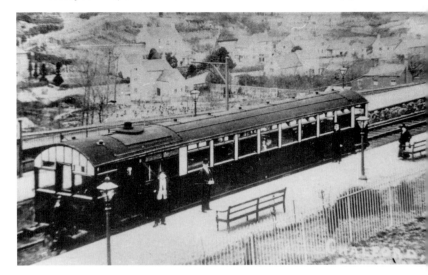

Steam railmotor No. 2 at the Down platform, Chalford. The chimney can be seen towards the front. Author's collection

An up auto train at Chalford in the nineteen-thirties. Author's collection

A push-pull to Gloucester awaits departure from Chalford 10 October 1948. L. E. Copeland

In 1908 the Chalford Temperance Society wait for their train to Weston super Mare. They will travel all the way on the GWR via Swindon. Author's collection

GWR bus CO 84, a 20 h.p. Milnes-Daimler, at the Chalford terminus 31 March 1905. It was first licensed, at Plymouth, 18 May 1904. Author's collection

Railmotor tickets.

Chalford: view from the up end of the platform 10 October 1948. Beyond the signal box an auto train awaits its next turn. L. E. Copeland

Chalford yard and the rear of the Up side building August 1963. 14XX class 0–4–2T No. 1455 about to cross from the Up to the Down line. Author's collection

Chalford, view Down 24 April 1962. A hand crane is just visible in the goods yard. Author

14XX class 0–4–2T No. 1472 at Chalford with the 11.40 a.m. Chalford to Gloucester Central 18 April 1963. Author

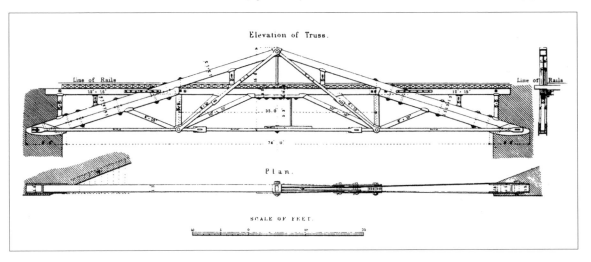

St Mary's Viaduct: a combination of Oregon pine and wrought iron.

The St Mary's Viaduct a single span of 74 feet across the Thames & Severn Canal stretched the timber form to the limit. St Mary's Crossing Halt (98 miles 62 chains), with wooden platforms and a corrugated iron shelter, was immediately beyond, opened 12 October 1903, a small booking office being fitted below the steps of St Mary's Crossing signal box. A footbridge was erected following the death of a young woman crossing to St Mary's Mill.

Brimscombe (99 miles 24 chains) opened 1 June 1845 had a neat, stone-built, Brunellan chalet-type station and stone goods shed with timber ends. The Up refuge siding holding 54 wagons was cut into the embankment to keep it level so it was necessarily above the main line at its west end. A footbridge was built in 1898 when a young lady using the public footpath level crossing from the main road to Wimberley Mills was killed by a train. The original small signal box was at the west end of the Down platform, but siding traffic grew to such an extent that a new West box was built in July 1896 and an East box on the Up platform, near the locomotive shed in 1898. Brimscombe West box was only opened for shunting. An Up train wishing to stop for water at Kemble was required to give one long whistle followed by three shorts when passing Brimscombe East signal box. The Victoria Inn opposite the station and formerly patronised by crews of banking engines, was renamed the 'King & Castle' in 1985 — inappropriate as in the steam era Kings were banned from this route. However in GWR days, No. 6028 *King George VI* arrived at Gloucester with an express diverted because of Severn Tunnel repairs and it is believed that it clipped the Down platform at Cashes Green en route. In the nineteen-sixties a King visited Gloucester in error and was then sent to Bristol on the Midland route via Yate. Brimscombe station closed to freight traffic on 12 August 1963, and passengers 2 November 1964.

Beyond Brimscombe is the 168-yards-long Bourne Viaduct, one 67 foot span over the canal and 16 others varying from 18 to 30 feet. The canal span was made up of three timber trusses each of which consisted of a triangular king truss, with an internal trapezoidal queen truss. The inclined timbers, or principal beams, rested in iron shoes on the piers, while the upper horizontal beam of the queen truss carried the roadway planking which was continued on beams supported by the principals. The timbers carrying the roadway received support from struts radiating from the feet of the queen posts which were connected with the apex of the king truss by iron ties.

The Down platform St Mary's Crossing Halt *c.* 1960. The platform is unusually narrow. The actual crossing is between the platform ramp and the signal box. Lens of Sutton

St Mary's Crossing Halt view Up *c.* 1960. Lens of Sutton

St Mary's Crossing signal box 7 May 1933. Tickets are sold in the hut below the stairs. In the event of fire, the signalman has two escape routes! L.E. Copeland

14XX class 0–4–2T No. 1409 with the 10.28 a.m. Gloucester Central to Chalford auto train approaches St Mary's Crossing Halt 24 April 1962. Due to the curvature of the line, for easy sighting the signal is on the opposite to normal. Brimscombe station is in the distance. Author

Above: 64XX class 0–6–0PT No. 6412 approaches St Mary's Crossing Halt 25 August 1964. No. 6412 is preserved. Rev. Alan Newman

Left: Telephone and 'Beware of Trains' notice at St Mary's Crossing box, 28 May 1991. Author

St Mary's Crossing, 28 May 1991. Author

An Up train headed by a 2–6–2T, having worked 'wrong line' from Stroud, regains the correct road by Chalford locomotive shed, 5 May 1935. The Thames & Severn Canal is on the right. The signal post is of concrete. L.E. Copeland

A 2–6–0 hauling a Down stopping train passes Brimscombe locomotive shed *c.* 1935. A 2–6–2T for banking stands outside the shed. M. J. Tozer

Ex-LMS Class 8F 2–8–0 No. 48739 calls at Brimscombe for water 14 June 1962. Immediately to its right is the timber pump house with the locomen's mess room beyond. Rev. Alan Newman

A steam railmotor bound for Chalford leaves Brimscombe. This card is postmarked 28.4.08. Author's collection

A 14XX class 0–4–2T propels two auto cars into Brimscombe on a Chalford to Gloucester working. Dr Christopher Kent

Brimscombe, view Up
16 April 1938. Empty milk
churns stand on the platform
— by this date they had
almost fallen out of fashion.
The locomotive shed is
beyond the signal box.
L. E. Copeland

Brimscombe, view Down
16 April 1938 showing the
goods shed. L. E. Copeland

Brimscombe, view Down
24 April 1962 Author

An unusual locomotive works a Chalford to Gloucester Central train — a 'Large' 2–6–2T, which, not being equipped for auto working, had to run round its coach at Chalford. Author's collection

5101 class 2–6–2T No. 4100 at Brimscombe 14 June 1962 between banking duties. Rev. Alan Newman

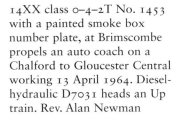

14XX class 0–4–2T No. 1453 with a painted smoke box number plate, at Brimscombe propels an auto coach on a Chalford to Gloucester Central working 13 April 1964. Diesel-hydraulic D7031 heads an Up train. Rev. Alan Newman

4–6–0 No. 5042 *Winchester Castle* (81A Old Oak Common), newly out-shopped from Swindon Works and on a running-in turn, shunts a goods train at Brimscombe 14 June 1962. The locomotive was withdrawn in June 1965. Rev. Alan Newman

2884 class 2–8–0 No. 3858 heads a Down goods past No. 5082 *Winchester Castle* at Brimscombe 14 June 1962. Rev. Alan Newman

14XX class 0–4–2T No. 1409 accelerates a Chalford to Gloucester Central auto train past No. 5082 *Winchester Castle* 14 June 1962. Rev. Alan Newman

A nineteen-thirties trade card depicting the GW & LMS Railways joint delivery 3-ton Scammell 3-wheeled mechanical horse based at Stroud. Author's collection

Brimscombe Bridge Halt (99 miles 74 chains) opened 1 February 1904, the platforms being staggered, the Down to the east of the bridge and the Up to the west. It was particularly used by the employees of two large cloth weaving mills.The bridge and a short tunnel about 10 feet in length are side by side. The halt, like others on the line, closed 2 November 1964.

Ham Mill Crossing Halt (100 miles 64 chains) opened 12 October 1903 and proved useful for workers at a nearby carpet factory and engineering works. Electric treadles and bells were fitted both sides of the level crossing warning passengers and persons crossing the railway of a train's approach. Similar equipment was also fitted at Bowbridge, Ebley and Downfield Crossings. Bowbridge Crossing Halt (101 miles 37 chains) opened 1 May 1905 was near a large dye works. Immediately before Stroud is Capel's Viaduct, 253 yards of eighteen 30-foot spans, followed by Canal Viaduct of one span over the Stroudwater Canal and three others of 38 feet, 28 feet and 22 feet.

Stroud (102 miles 13 chains) is a major station. The stone building had its ticket office modernised in the summer of 1975. Two Barlow rails placed back to back form gateposts almost opposite the goods shed which still bears the initials GWR. Trains wishing to run via the Cheltenham Loop at Gloucester South junction were required to give one long whistle and two shorts to the Stroud signalman. Adjacent to the Down platform were two water tanks, a circular one on a round stone base and a cuboid on pillars. Possibly the latter was added when the introduction of railmotors increased the volume of water required.

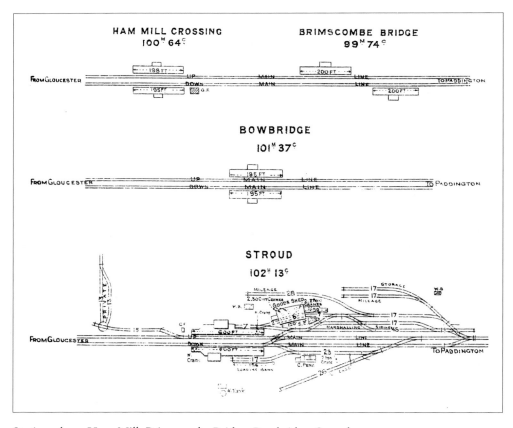

Station plans: Ham Mill, Brimscombe Bridge, Bowbridge, Stroud.

Brimscombe Bridge Halt *c.* 1903. It appears as if a vehicle has run out of control down the hill and crashed into the railway cutting. Just behind the platform fencing can be seen a vehicle chassis and one wheel. Michael Farr collection

Brimscombe Bridge Halt 9 October 1950. The earlier timber platform has been replaced by a solid structure and a corrugated iron pagoda erected. The tunnel immediately abuts the bridge. Author's collection

A 'banner' signal south of Brimscombe Bridge taken from the front of a DMU, 13 June 1988. Author

The Down platform of Brimscombe Bridge Halt viewed through the tunnel which is only about 10 feet in length. The Up platform is in the foreground. Lens of Sutton

Bowbridge Crossing Halt, view Up *c.* 1961. Electric lighting has been installed; the lamp posts are very tall. Lens of Sutton

Bowbridge Crossing Halt sign. Author's collection

Stroud station *c.* 1850. Author's collection

The bridge carrying the GWR over the Thames & Severn Canal, 31 July 1985. Beyond is the Midland Railway bridge taking a carriageway to the MR station. Author

Building set in an arch of Capel's Viaduct *c.* 1990. John Mann

Stroud: the extensive goods yard, view Down towards the passenger station, 15 June 1946. L. E. Copeland

View Down from the signal box 15 June 1946. 'Stroud' on the goods shed was blackened out as a WW2 measure to make it difficult for possible invaders to locate themselves. L.E. Copeland

Interesting track work on Capel's Viaduct 12 July 1984. The distance from Paddington — 101 miles 50½ chains — is painted on the end of the bridge parapet. John Mann

View Up from the end of the passenger station, 15 June 1946. On the left is a water crane, goods shed and signal box. L. E. Copeland

The splendid goods shed, 3 August 1981, with the goods offices, left. Author

Another view of the goods shed 31 July 1985. Author

Owing to the enormous increase in local passenger traffic consequent upon the opening of the railmotor service, the platforms became inconveniently overcrowded on Saturdays and market days, so in 1913 the buildings on the Down side were demolished, set back and both platforms lengthened. One interesting feature is a tree on the Down platform. When the station opened in April 1845 there was a plantation of trees and shrubs at the back of the Down platform. Untouched at first, as traffic requirements grew, trees had to be felled to make room for new buildings. Alterations to the station in 1890 included extensions to the platform, but this American beech was left standing just behind the Down platform railings. It formed a welcome shade on a hot day and a seat was placed to take advantage of the tree's shelter. Extensions in 1913–14 included shifting the fence, so brought the tree on the platform itself. At this time its future was in the balance and there was much talk of felling the tree to create more space. People appealed and it was spared, a seat being built right round the trunk. During the Second World War United States troops collected seeds to take 'back home' and plant as a momento. It is an American fern leaf beech tree, *polypodum phegopteris*, uncommon in this country and about 160 years old.

The Number of Passengers Booked from Stroud

Year	No. of Passengers	Passenger Receipts
1868	49,597	8,773
1888	73,309	10,064
1889	81,482	10,783

The American beech on the platform. 4-6-0 No. 5988 *Bostock Hall* heads a Down stopping train. Author's collection

View Down *c.* 1946, cattle wagons stand on the left. Author's collection

The Up platform and footbridge *c.* 1946. Author's collection

View Down *c.* 1946. Author's collection

The exterior of the Up side 3 August 1981. Author

The exterior of the Down side, 3 August 1981. On the left is the American beech. Author

Steam railmotor No. 5 at Stroud *c.* 1908. Author's collection

64XX class 0–6–0PT No. 6437 taking on water. It is working the 10.45 a.m. Gloucester Central to Chalford 24 April 1962. Author

DMU W51450/51522 working the 11.35 Cheltenham to Swindon 3 August 1981. Author

Bert Holmes in Stroud signal box 9 September 1934. Author's collection

The interior of Stroud signal box November 1966. D. Payne

At the west end of the station is Watt's Viaduct (named after the brewers) 132 yards in length consisting of eight 30-foot spans and four stone arches. Beyond the viaduct a siding led to R. Townsend's Stratford Mill. With access over a wagon turntable, the Station Foreman was required to see personally that the turntable was set for the dead end before a movement was made into or out of the siding. Between the turntable and cattle food factory rolling stock was horse drawn. Stratford Viaduct 73 yards in length had one 40 foot and seven 30-foot spans.

Downfield Crossing Halt (102 miles 72 chains) opened 12 October 1903 and platforms and a corrugated iron shelter were erected circa 1921. Carpenter's (or Cainscross) Viaduct 47 yards, has four 32-foot spans.

Cashes Green Halt (103 miles 23 chains) opened on 21 January 1930 by public request to serve a housing estate. It had timber, later concrete, platforms each with a corrugated iron shelter.

Ebley Crossing Halt (103 miles 52 chains) opened 12 October 1903, originally with a timber platform and corrugated iron pagoda on the Up platform, latterly had the platforms replaced in concrete and a shelter erected on the Down platform too.

Jefferies' Siding and signal box (104 miles 29 chains) opened 26 July 1898 to serve a brick works. The signal box closed, the crossover from the Down line removed and a ground frame installed late in 1936, the siding being recovered 27 November 1960.

Stonehouse (Burdett Road) (104 miles 75 chains) had its station offices built of stone as was the goods shed. At one time the Stonehouse Brick & Tile Works stood at the Up end of the station and provided the line with traffic, coal arriving and bricks being despatched. Standish Hospital had all its coal sent to the station, carts collecting daily, while Gloucestershire County Council had coal delivered there for its steam rollers. A Saturday morning task for permanent way men was tidying up the yard, brick yard siding and the two coal sidings.

In 1974 the local populace was delighted when BR decided to reprieve the station and voted a parish rate of 2p in the pound to raise more than £8,000 towards the £13,500 cost of repairs. BR announced improved services to the station including the first Sunday trains for years. Then a bombshell fell when it was announced that the station was to be closed on 6 October 1975, BR claiming that it had not the finance to carry out repairs because the Department of the Environment had listed the building as being of historic or architectural interest. BR had intended renovating just the booking hall and waiting rooms and demolishing the remaining buildings, but listing prevented this and meant that the project would cost £30,000. In the event, the Department of the Environment agreed to demolition and rebuilding in a different style, the uninteresting stone boxes being completed in the spring of 1977. Until this rebuilding, the height of the Down platform was sub-standard in front of the station building.

Standish Junction (106 miles 51 chains), where the Bristol & Gloucester and CGWUR lines met and ran parallel to Gloucester, has enjoyed quite a history. The first junction, opened on 8 July 1844, closed on 19 May 1854 when the MR opened its independent standard gauge line; the second junction opened on 21 April 1873, following the abolition of standard gauge in the Gloucester area, to allow the Great Western to exercise its running powers over the MR, and lasted until 1887; while the third junction opened on 25 July 1908 in order that the GWR's Birmingham to Bristol expresses via the new Honeybourne line could use the MR between Standish and Yate. Junction expenses, including the signalman's wages, were shared by the two companies. For trains coming south on to the Bristol line it was practice that the first train past Naas Crossing signal box had precedence. In order to hold goods trains awaiting a path forward over either line, the GWR opened two goods sidings on the Up side north of the Junction on 26 September 1943.

Right: Watts' Viaduct 15 June 1946 and the centrally-pivoted signals taking less room in a limited space. At the Down end of the viaduct R. Townsend's siding diverges to the right. Author's collection

Below: Watts' Viaduct, view Down 3 August 1981. Author

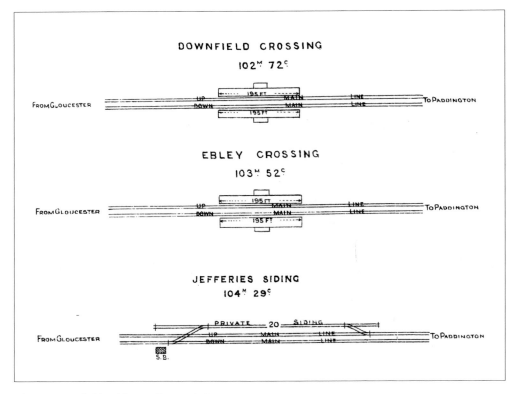

Plans: Downfield, Ebley, Jefferies' Siding.

The boiler end of steam railmotor No. 2 at an unidentified halt in the Stroud Valley. Notice the burnished cylinder covers. Author's collection

Right: The gate keeper's hut at Beard's Lane Crossing 21 January 1937. L. E. Copeland

Below: No. 2 steam railmotor at Downfield Crossing Halt. Only the able-bodied could manage the steps. The conductor is on the right. Author's collection

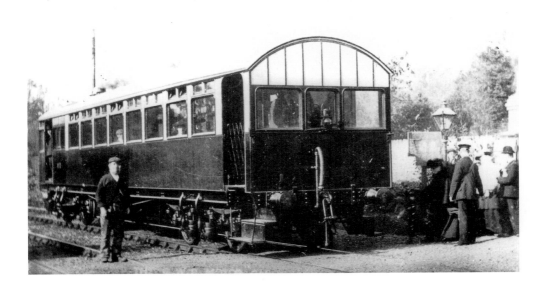

Downfield Crossing Halt view Up 24 April 1962. Author

14XX class 0–4–2T No. 1409 with the 11.45 a.m. Chalford to Gloucester Central propels a modern auto trailer at Downfield Crossing Halt 24 April 1962. Author

Cashes Green Halt view Up
28 November 1957.
L. E. Copeland

14XX class 0–4–2T No.
1441 at Cashes Green Halt
with a Gloucester Central
to Chalford working 28
November 1957.
L. E. Copeland

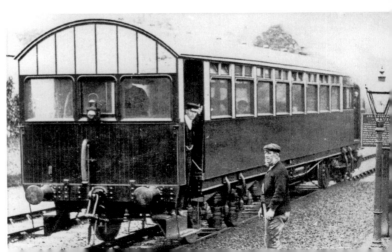

A steam railmotor at Ebley
Crossing Halt before the
platforms were built. The
steps on the early railmotors
were fixed; the later design
had them retractable. Author's
collection

Above: Steam railmotor No. 50 on an Up working at Ebley Crossing Halte (notice the early spelling) No. 50 came to Gloucester in 1908. Author's collection

Left: Steam railmotor No. 48 at Ebley Crossing Halt. It first arrived at Gloucester in 1908, but left the following year. It was destroyed in the fire at Chalford in January 1916. Author's collection

Ebley Crossing Halt was modernised with concrete components and corrugated iron shelters of less attractive design than the original pagodas. Electric lighting has been installed. View Up 11 May 1961. Author

14XX class 0–4–2T No. 1444 calls at Ebley Crossing Halt with the 13.03 Gloucester Central to Chalford 22 August 1964. Autocar W242W is one of the modern vehicles built in 1953. R. E. Toop

A Swindon 'Cross-Country' DMU approaches Ebley Crossing Halt 28 November 1957. The blind reads 'Special' suggesting that it is on a drivers' training run from Swindon, or running for test purposes. L. E. Copeland

NOTICE No. 1739.

TUESDAY, JULY 26th.

New Signal Box and Siding between Stonehouse Station and Beards Lane Crossing.

On **Tuesday, July 26th,** between the hours of **6 a.m.** and **5.30 p.m.**, the Signal Department will connect the points and Signals to the Signal Box provided for working the new Siding to be known as "Jefferies Siding," situated between Stonehouse Station and Beards Lane Crossing.

The Signal Box, Signals and Sidings will not be brought into use until further notice.

New Signals as follows :—

FORM.	NAME.	POSITION.	DISTANCE FROM BOX.
	Down Main Distant.	Down Side of Line.	860 yards.
	1 Down Main Home. 2 Down Main Distant for Stonehouse.	Ditto	15 yards.
	1 Down Main Starting. 2 Down Main Repeating Distant for Stonehouse.	Ditto	350 yards.
	Up Main Starting.	Ditto	350 yards.
	Up Main Home.	Up Side of Line.	65 yards.
	1 Up Main Advanced Starting for Stonehouse. 2 Up Distant for Jefferies Siding.	Ditto	570 yards.

Discs will be fixed at the Points leading from Siding and at the Points of Crossover Road.

The following Signals will be taken out of use at Stonehouse at the same time :—

Down Main Distant.   Down Main Repeating Distant.   Up Advanced Starting.

All arrangements for safe working of the line (including appointment of any Groundmen to be made by Inspector Kirk in accordance with Rule 71.)

T. WAINWRIGHT,
Divisional Superintendent.

Hereford,
July 20th, 1898.

Left: Official notice of the opening of Jefferies' Siding and signal box.

Below: Misspelt ticket (left) and a road motor ticket (right) issued at Stroud.

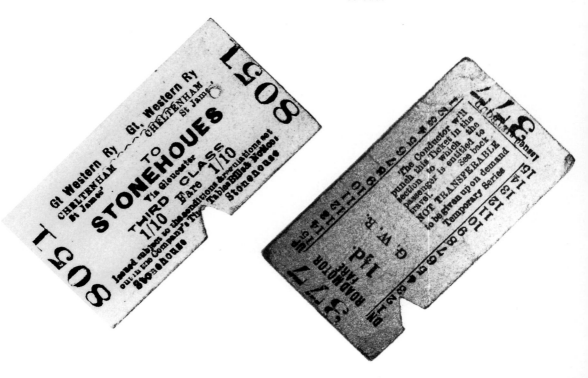

An Up stopping train draws into Stonehouse *c.* 1910. Author's collection

Stonehouse, view Up 1921. Notice the low platform in front of the station building, right. This would have been the original level. Author's collection

The Down end of the fine goods shed at Stonehouse. On the left is MR wagon No. 200820. Author's collection

Goods and brick works sidings at Stonehouse *c.* 1914, view Up. The sidings on the left are on longitudinal sleepers. Author's collection

Stonehouse *c.* 1906 with the Stonehouse Brick & Tile Co Ltd's works in the background. Author's collection

Stonehouse, Burdett Road view Down 11 May 1961. New sleepers on the platform are probably for partial track relaying, or replacements for rotten specimens. Author

The Up side building at Stonehouse in the mid-nineteen seventies. A poster announces fare increases. Michael Farr

The Up side building at Stonehouse in the mid-nineteen seventies. The boarded signal box closed 5 October 1970. Michael Farr

Right: Signalman Cyril Minnet at Stonehouse, 1968. Cyril Minnet collection

Below: DMU set No. L404 at the Down platform, Stonehouse, before the station was rebuilt. Michael Farr

DMU set No. C823 enters Stonehouse working the 12.00 Swindon to Worcester 29 August 1985. Author

Rear view of DMU C823 working the 12.00 Swindon to Worcester 29 August 1985. Author

Stonehouse, view Down 3 August 1981 showing the new buildings. Author

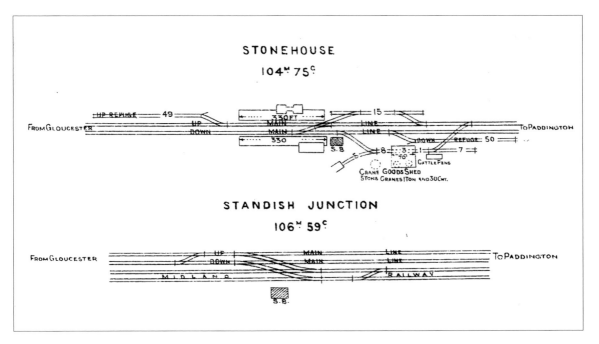

Plans: Stonehouse, Standish Junction.

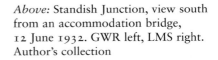

Above: Standish Junction, view south
from an accommodation bridge,
12 June 1932. GWR left, LMS right.
Author's collection

Left: Standish Junction view north
21 January 1937, GWR right, LMS left.
Author's collection

Above: Standish Junction signal box 26 February 1967. D Payne

Right: Signalman Cyril Minnet in Standish Junction signal box, 1947. Cyril Minnet collection

Standish Junction 29 August 1985. The gas cylinders are for point heaters. Author

14XX class 0–4–2T No. 1440 working the 3.06 p.m. Gloucester Central to Chalford at Standish, 11 May 1961. Author

At Standish February 1964 BR Standard class 5 4–6–0 No. 73164 heads a Bristol to Gloucester Eastgate stopping train. It is about to pass an up freight to Stroud hauled by a 94XX class 0–6–0PT. W. F. Grainger

On 26 October 1964 another Junction, Standish North (106 miles 67 chains) was laid so that trains in either direction on the Swindon to Gloucester line could use the former LMSR line. As part of the Gloucester MAS reorganisation, from 8 September 1968 the line from Gloucester to Standish became just two tracks, the actual junction being at 106 miles 67 chains and a new ground frame and crossover sited 3 chains beyond. Between 24-26 February 1997 the junction was remodelled at a cost of £2m allowing the maximum speed to be raised from 40 to 100 mph.

Haresfield station only had platforms on the MR lines and the MR alone served the National Shell Filling Factory sidings, together with its single platform on a special branch. The sidings completed on 1 June 1916 were removed in December 1925. The approximate site came into use again on 9 April 1939 as Quedgeley Depot, these sidings are now lifted. A train for Gloucester New Yard was required to give one crow whistle followed by two shorts to the signalman at Naas Crossing. In the 1955 BR Modernisation Plan Gloucester was seen as being a sorting point for South Wales and South West traffic and it was intended to open a marshalling yard covering the fields between the main line and Brookthorpe. The project was officially abandoned in August 1964 due to the policy of withdrawing much wagon-load traffic and the closure of so many minor goods stations. With the introduction of the Gloucester MAS scheme, Naas Crossing signal box became Brookthorpe Crossing signal box on 15 September 1968, the gates continuing to be worked from the former signal box. On 20 May 1977 a fire destroyed part of the box roof and as the building was life expired, it was replaced by a new cabin brought into use on 24 July 1977 with outside ground frame and Annett's Key release for the gate levers. Subsequently the crossing has been replaced by a new road to the south using a former occupation underline bridge, the level crossing now being only for a footpath.

2884 class 2–8–0 No. 3820 with an Up express freight not fitted with continuous brakes, waits at Standish Junction for a path, 11 May 1961. Author

4–6–0 No. 4990 *Clifton Hall* with an Up parcels train south of Haresfield 11 May 1961. Author

Diesel-hydraulic D6327 with the 2.40 p.m. Gloucester Central to Swindon at Haresfield 1 May 1961. Author

Haresfield station 11 May 1961 view north on the ex-LMS line. It is illuminated by oil lamps. The former GWR tracks are beyond the fence on the right. Author

The south junction of Quedgeley Sidings. View from rear of a Cheltenham to Swindon DMU 16 June 1988. The mile post marks 97 miles from Derby. The left window reflects part of the coach. Author

The north junction of Quedgeley Sidings 13 June 1988. Author

Chequers Road Junction (113 miles 2 chains) is the bifurcation of the line to Gloucester passenger station and that to Cheltenham, the former curving past New Yard and the former Gloucester Railway Carriage & Wagon Works, (now a housing estate), to Tramway Junction (113 miles 55 chains), site of the Gloucester MAS box opened 25 May 1968. This is adjacent to Horton Road, (or Asylum Lane as it was then known), level crossing, an interesting spot as it was here that the broad gauge Cheltenham line crossed the standard gauge Birmingham & Gloucester Railway and also the horse-worked Cheltenham & Gloucester Railway, the level crossing gates being set no less than 58 yards apart.

As work on the Birmingham & Gloucester Railway was more advanced than that of the CGWUR, it was agreed that the Birmingham company should purchase the site for a station at Gloucester (114 miles 9 chains) and sell to the Cheltenham company three acres on the north side of its station at cost price when the latter required it. The CGWUR station, on the site of today's Gloucester station, had two platforms with a centre siding for coach stabling, the three lines being linked by turntable at the terminal end. The other GWR station at Gloucester was the T station opened on 23 October 1847 west of the present Eastern Avenue and situated at the point where a short single line from Gloucester station crossed the Avoiding Line, (giving a direct run from Swindon to Cheltenham), at right angles, connecting with it by means of a turntable in each of the running lines and terminating in a short dead end beyond. Because of the configuration of the short line and the avoiding line, it became known as the 'T station' and the short single line from the existing Great Western station was the 'T line'. A shuttle service worked by former 2–2–2 tender engines converted to the tank variety was run over the T line to connect with trains running directly to and from Cheltenham, Gloucester vehicles being transferred by turntable.

The Engineman's Rule Book of 1848 stipulated: '*All trains passing along the Main (or Avoiding) Line at Gloucester must stop before reaching the Turn-table, unless the Engineman sees that the T Line Engine has gone across and is standing on the opposite side of the line, and unless he also receives the Signal from the Policeman.*' This unusual method of working Gloucester traffic continued until the South Wales Railway was opened in 1851 when a curve was built by Chequers Bridge to a new through station situated north of that of the CGWUR which was now sandwiched between the South Wales Railway and the Birmingham line. The T station closed 19 September 1851 and the avoiding line became derelict, the track not being lifted until 1872, although the T station house lasted until September 1971 when it was bulldozed to make room for sidings alongside the avoiding line. The South Wales station, originally with Up and Down platforms, by 1855 had the Up platform removed to make more room for sidings, the former Down platform being lengthened and taking in the site of the former CGWUR terminus. It was used for trains in both directions and had the advantage of avoiding passengers and their luggage having to cross lines. Down trains used the west end and Up trains the east end, a scissors crossover being placed midway along the platform. Eventually to ease working, an Up platform was built in 1899.

When the Midland terminus adjacent to the GWR station was replaced by a station at Eastgate on 12 April 1896, a long covered footbridge 250 yards in length connected the GWR and MR stations to facilitate interchange. In 1919 Gloucester station became 'closed' with the consequent result that the bridge could only be used by ticket holders, this leading to criticism as inhabitants on the north side of Gloucester were unable to use the bridge to reach the MR station, or those on the south side to reach the GWR station, some citizens complaining of this being unjust treatment as the building of the bridge was a compromise when a joint station could not be opened. By this time the GWR station at Gloucester had grown to an important size. The four through roads consisted of two platform lines and two centre roads, the 'up and down middle'. The Down platform marked Nos 2 & 3, was bisected by a scissors crossing connecting with the Down middle line, in order that a Down train could be routed into Platform No. 2 when No. 3 was occupied, or an engine released from Platform No. 3 when No. 2 was busy, this only applying to short trains, longer ones occupying both platforms. The Up platform was similarly divided by a scissors crossing into Platforms Nos 4 & 5. The Up bay was No. 6 and the Down, or Hereford bay, No. 1.

The GWR station at Gloucester, view east *c.* 1850. Notice the unusually long platform. George Measom

The T Station house, Gloucester. Here passengers from Gloucester changed trains to Swindon. Dr A. J. G. Dickens

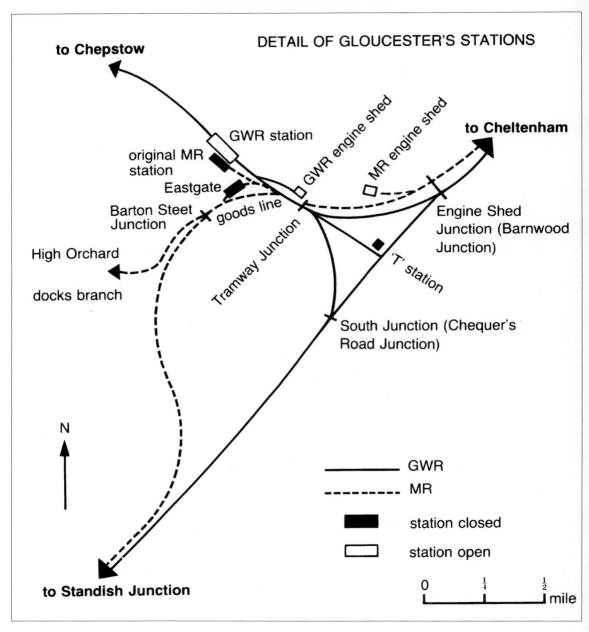

DETAIL OF GLOUCESTER'S STATIONS

to Chepstow

GWR station

original MR station

Eastgate

Barton Steet Junction

High Orchard

docks branch

goods line

Tramway Junction

GWR engine shed

MR engine shed

to Cheltenham

Engine Shed Junction (Barnwood Junction)

'T' station

South Junction (Chequer's Road Junction)

N

to Standish Junction

GWR

MR

station closed

station open

0   ¼   ½

mile

Gloucester stations.

Gloucester *c.* 1905, view west. A 0–6–0 heads the Up stopping train. Notice the 'scissors' crossover enabling the long platform to be used by two trains simultaneously. The Middle signal box, closed 31 July 1931, peeps above the roof, left. The signal arms are supported in an unusual way. Author's collection

A Down express at the far end of Gloucester station *c.* 1905. Author's collection

Brand new Star class 4–6–0 No. 4023 *King George* at Gloucester with the up Royal train 23 June 1909. Notice the crowns on the two lower headlights. For safety the points have been clamped to prevent a movement facing the Royal train. The signal box can be seen above the platform canopy. Etches

Empty platforms at Gloucester Central, view east. Notice the lamp by the left-hand water column to facilitate taking on water in the dark. Lens of Sutton

The travelling safe from Stroud on Platform 2, 26 June 1986. The box had a double trap, no-return lid and travelled in the guard's compartment daily. Author

4–6–0 No. 4079 *Pendennis Castle* at Tramway Crossing, 13 May 1950 with a Paddington to Cheltenham express. No. 4079 has been preserved. W. Potter

4–6–0 No. 5017 *The Gloucestershire Regiment 28ᵗʰ 61ˢᵗ* leaving Gloucester Central 25 March 1961. The regimental badge is displayed on the splasher below the nameplate. Michael Jenkins

5101 class 2–6–2T No. 4107 on station pilot duty, Gloucester Central 22 August 1964. R. E. Toop

72XX class 2–8–2T No. 7250 at Gloucester Central with an Up freight passing 14XX class 0–4–2T No. 1441 (85B Gloucester Horton Road) with the 2.40 p.m. Saturdays-only auto train Cheltenham St James' to Chalford 16 May 1959. R. E. Toop

One particularly interesting and unique feature of the GWR goods yard at Gloucester was that it was served by a branch of the Gloucester Corporation's electric tramway. During the First World War an aerodrome and aircraft factory were built at Brockworth. It was decided to extend the Hucclecote tramway route for rather more than half a mile on a private right of way along the north side of the road, so that it could serve these premises for both passengers and goods traffic. Because of a wartime shortage of materials, the little-used Westgate Street section was lifted in 1917 and the track and overhead equipment salvaged to build the new extension opened later that year. A siding was laid from London Road along Great Western Road to the GWR goods yard. This temporary track was laid on the surface of the road and fenced off. Double deck tram No. 14 had a framework fitted to both sides enabling it to carry aircraft propellers vertically and pulled wagons containing other supplies. As the gauge was 3 feet 6 inches ordinary railway wagons could not be used so special ones were built in the Corporation's workshops. Initially the tramway was used up to 20 hours a day, first for the conveyance of materials for constructing the aerodrome and factory, and then for the conveyance of aircraft parts. In addition to goods traffic, the tramway extension to Brockworth carried 1,200 to 1,300 workers daily, but after the war was used only for the occasional goods traffic. In the summer of 1922 a regular public passenger service was started to the Victoria Hotel, Brockworth, but as traffic did not develop as anticipated, the extension was abandoned on 1 October 1924. The temporary track had been removed from Great Western Road towards the end of 1920.

The opening of a new GWR line from Honeybourne, south of Stratford-upon-Avon to Cheltenham in 1906 meant that the GWR was able to inaugurate a new route from Birmingham to Bristol and the South West. To obviate the delay of reversing trains at Gloucester, the avoiding line was relaid and opened to goods on 25 November 1901 and to passengers on 1 July 1906. There was talk of opening a station at Chequers

Bridge to facilitate north to south trains stopping at Gloucester without need for reversal, but this scheme never came to fruition. In November 1964, when new crossovers were installed at Standish Junction to allow Paddington to Cheltenham trains a straight run through to the Eastgate station, it was envisaged that the Central station, as it was re-named on 17 September 1951, would be converted into a parcels depot. South Wales trains would be accommodated at Eastgate by constructing a new curved platform link to the Central tracks. Then, in 1968 plans were drafted for building a completely new £150,000 station at Barnwood, but eventually this idea was dropped, partly on cost and partly because of the site's remoteness from the bus station and commercial centre. Eventually it was decided to close Eastgate station as this would allow the removal of five busy and costly to operate level crossings and also because of the high development value of land occupied by that route between the station and Tuffley Junction.

Although Eastgate station and the line serving it closed on 1 December 1975 and the buildings at Central demolished and replaced by temporary portable buildings, the rebuilt Central station was not officially opened by the Mayor, Councillor Terry Wathen, until 8 March 1977. The redevelopment cost £1½ m, £1m of which covered the track layout and signalling. Traffic was once again concentrated on what was the Down platform which was lengthened to 1,600ft, becoming the second longest in the country. The former Up platform was relegated to parcels use but was brought back into passenger use in 1984 as Platform No. 4. Still complete with its Great Western ironwork it is linked with Platform Nos 1 — 3 by means of a new metal footbridge. Platform 1, is the east end of the former Down platform, Platform 2 the west end of the former Down platform and No. 3 the Newport bay, also used by postal and newspaper trains.

The exterior of the rebuilt Gloucester Central station, 26 June 1986. Author

Right: Paving imitating railway track, outside of Gloucester station 17 April 1996. Author

Below: Opening plaque. Author

DMU No. 150249 at Platform 3 with the 13.22 to Swindon, 17 April 1996. Author

Gloucester 26 June 1986: left, No. 31186 with an Up freight of wire coils, while DMU B437 arrives at Platform 2 with the 09.27 Cheltenham to Swindon. Author

Gloucester 17 April 1996: DMU No. 150249 left with the 13.22 to Swindon and right, DMU No. 158837 working the 12.15 Cardiff to Birmingham. Both trains are in Regional Railways livery. Author

DMU B437 at Platform 2 with the 10.42 Swindon to Cheltenham 26 June 1986. Author

DMU B437 at Platform 2 with the 09.27 Cheltenham to Swindon 26 June 1986. The indicator box has been blanked off out of use. Author

In the mid-1950s, when Gloucester received 130 tons of goods daily, parcel handling was mechanised by the installation of a 280-foot-long conveyor belt. Packages were conveyed label uppermost and the parcels removed at the appropriate cartage post, placed on a road vehicle and checked. As far as possible articulated road vehicles were used so that the trailers could be loaded while the tractor units worked elsewhere. After unloading, the empty rail wagons were moved on by capstan and the next four vehicles drawn into position for unloading.

Train Services

Curves and gradients prevented fast running over the line, apart from the 'racing' stretch Tuffley Junction to Standish Junction where the line ran parallel with the Midland. Opening from Swindon to Cirencester saw a service of six Down and seven Up trains. With the opening to Gloucester there was a service of eight trains each way, ordinary trains running from Paddington to Gloucester in 4½ hours, the express being scheduled to cover the distance of 114 miles in 2 hours 55 minutes.

In 1887 the fastest train from Paddington covered the distance in 2 hours 52 minutes — an improvement of 3 minutes in 42 years. That year the fastest train from Swindon to Gloucester stopping only at Kemble and Stroud took 1 hour 3 minutes. Nine trains ran each way, most of which stopped at all stations. Although back in 1879 nine Up and eight Down trains ran daily, all but two each way carrying third class passengers, there was but one Up and one Down train by which Stroud passengers could travel third class. This was so arranged as to prevent a passenger going and returning the same day. Matters had improved by 1914, a contributor to the

Railway & Travel Monthly writing: *Stroud enjoys a remarkably fine train service to the metropolis. There are eleven Down and ten Up trains during the 24 hours. Many of these are expresses in every way, the fastest time between the two points being 2 hours 1 minute by the 2.54 pm ex Stroud with one stop at Kemble Junction, and 2 hours 18 minutes in the reverse direction by the 3.15 pm ex Paddington, stopping at Swindon and Kemble. In view of the long steep grade at Sapperton, the Up train's performance is distinctly meritorious. A highly popular train is the 8.5 am ex Stroud, which, for the convenience of dwellers higher up the valley, calls at Brimscombe at 8.12 am and reaches Paddington at 10.35 am. A breakfast car is run on this train. A very convenient corresponding Down train in the evening is the 6.10 pm ex Paddington, reaching Stroud at 8.35 pm, with dining car accommodation. These trains are very popular with Stroud Valley businessmen visiting London for the day. It is possible to reach Stroud as late as eight minutes past midnight from London, and to leave for the metropolis as late (or early) as 12.48 am.*

In 1924 the 8.00 a.m. Cheltenham to Paddington and 5.00 p.m. return were put on to compete with a new coach service and ran non-stop Stroud to Paddington. The train of five coaches was hauled by County class 4–4–0s.

By July 1938 eleven trains ran each way, the fastest Down being the Cheltenham Spa Express taking 2 hours 10 minutes not stopping at Swindon, but only at Kemble and Stroud. Its famous Up counterpart was put on as an afternoon service after the First

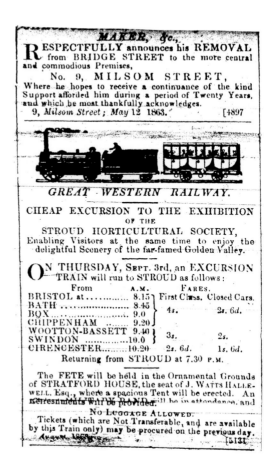

Advertisement in the *Bath & Cheltenham Gazette* 2 September 1863 for an excursion to the Golden Valley.

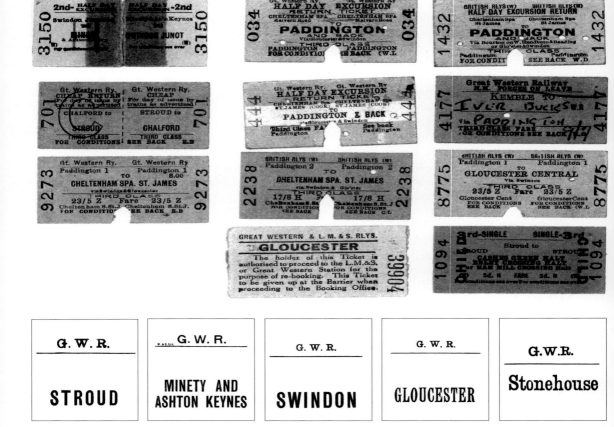

A selection of tickets and luggage labels.

World War and on 9 July 1923 was speeded up to capture the British record for the fastest run and unofficially known as the 'Cheltenham Flyer'. Speed over the Cotswolds was necessarily unspectacular, the record breaking section being between Swindon and Paddington. It left Cheltenham at 2.40 p.m. and from 1923 to 1926 at Gloucester South Junction the six coaches were joined by a brake composite from Hereford, the train being one of the very few from Cheltenham to London using the Gloucester avoiding line. The 'Cheltenham Flyer' never reappeared after the Second World War.

In the summer of 1957 nine Down and eight Up trains ran between Swindon and Gloucester including the 1.00 a.m. sleeping car train from Paddington to Carmarthen and its Up counterpart. The fastest train from Swindon to Gloucester took 55 minutes. From 2 November 1964 all Paddington to Cheltenham trains used Eastgate station to avoid reversal at Gloucester Central, reverting to Central when Eastgate closed and from this date, all the halts and four stations between Gloucester and Swindon were closed. From 7 October 1974 Sunday and new later weekday services called at Stonehouse. Two HSTs started running over the line from Swindon to Cheltenham in May 1983. The 2009 timetable shows 18 trains each way daily and 10 Up and 12 Down on Sundays.

On 12 October 1903 a local railmotor service began between Chalford and Stonehouse taking 23 minutes with six intermediate stops, running hourly 8.00 a.m. – 7.00 p.m. from Chalford and returning on the half hour from Stonehouse. Two late

Window label on the Cheltenham Spa Express — the 10.43 Paddington to Great Malvern, 26 June 1986. Passengers are warned that some stations, viz Stonehouse, Worcester Foregate Street, Malvern Link and Great Malvern have short platforms. Author

trains ran on Fridays and three on Saturdays. Following pressure from Stonehouse Parish Council, on 11 November 1912 an additional late train was tried Mondays to Wednesdays in addition to Thursdays to Saturdays for an experimental period of one month. At the end of the period the GWR sent a letter to the Council saying that although they would have liked to have seen it better patronised, it would continue running until further notice.

By 1922 the railmotors offered a half hourly interval service from 4.00 p.m. until 7.30 p.m. On 11 July 1921 the service was extended to Gloucester, though probably with auto trains rather than railmotors. In July 1938 there was an hourly service from Chalford to Stonehouse, leaving on the hour from 7.00 a.m., approximately every other train running through to Gloucester. On Saturdays a half hourly service was run in the late afternoon and early evening. By the summer of 1957 the regular interval service was beginning to disappear, trains only tending to leave Chalford on or about the hour. There were 14 auto trains each way, two running through to Kemble. Forty minutes were allowed from Chalford to Gloucester. The auto trains were withdrawn on 2 November 1964, it being appropriate that the first line on the GWR to have such a service, should also be the last on the WR. It offered a useful service which buses could not provide and sometimes as many as 10 or 12 prams would be parked down the centre of the coaches. Trains remained busy until withdrawal as buses took longer and charged higher fares.

Speed Restrictions 1945:
Junction at Swindon 30 mph
West portal Sapperton Tunnel to Brimscombe 40 mph (goods trains 20 mph)
Brimscombe to Stroud (Down trains) 45 mph
Standish Junction LMSR to GWR line 35 mph
Gloucester South Junction 40 mph
Gloucester South box 20 mph
Tramway Junction 10 mph

Possible Future Development

The present single line between Swindon and Kemble affects the track capacity — a serious factor as it is the primary diversionary route when the Severn Tunnel is closed for repair and when the South Wales line is electrified. The Great Western Route Utilisation Strategy (RUS) Draft for Consultation published in 2009, reviews what infrastructure requirements would be necessary to operate four trains per hour to accommodate future growth and for diversionary purposes. These consist of:

A) An hourly passenger service (either local or high speed service) between Swindon and Cheltenham Spa calling at Kemble, Stroud, Stonehouse and Gloucester. From 2016 this will be replaced with an IEP (Intercity Express Programme) train running a proposed hourly Paddington to Cheltenham service.

B) An hourly freight service between Swindon Loco Yard and Gloucester Yard Junction (assuming a Class 6 with 2000 tonnes trailing load).

C) Two Paddington to South Wales high speed services diverted when the Severn Tunnel is closed.

Doubling Swindon to Kemble was mentioned in a House of Commons debate on 30 June 2008, regarding delays due to the single track. The infrastructure failed to support an hourly timetable and delays were regularly exported from the line. Network Rail believed a significant demand from both passengers and freight was surpressed because of these limitations.

Passenger use of Kemble station had increased over 17 per cent annually. As the single track alignment was mainly central, it did not allow for a simple redoubling of the line. Network Rail estimated that the cost of doubling to be £32m and that such a scheme would have a benefit-to-cost ratio of 9.96 which placed it in the category of offering very good value for money. In addition to being a diversionary route for Severn Tunnel trains, it could provide a diversionary route for freight traffic from Southampton to the West Midlands and for trains from the South West to the North of England.

Another key cause for delay between Swindon and Kemble is the age of the track which needs regular repair. The current single line limits the amount of work that can be scheduled, whereas a doubled line would allow work to be undertaken more rapidly while maintaining a service.

A new station in the Moredon-Purton area would cater for the expanding North Swindon district. Without redoubling, the line could not see the benefits of the future IEP; doubling would facilitate the construction of a North Swindon station and the extra line capacity would permit additional local trains.

The Association of Train Operating Companies proposed an infill electrification including Swindon to Gloucester and Bristol to Birmingham. Were this to happen, all-electric IEP trains would be used Paddington to Cheltenham, rather than the hybrid combined diesel/electric versions now being considered.

The Route Utilisation Strategy is to look into the feasibility of a turn-back at Kemble for enhanced local services. Probably one of the main line platforms would have to be utilised for terminating trains, as the tight curvature of the former Cirencester branch platform would be unsuited to modern station design standards.

Cirencester Branch

To conclude the story of the Cirencester branch — it was closed for conversion to standard gauge on Wednesday 22 May 1872 and reopened on Monday 27 May. In the interim, passengers were conveyed by omnibus to and from Tetbury Road station, Kemble merely having platforms for changing trains with no access from outside. To reduce the costs of working the branch, on 2 February 1959 trains were replaced by a railbus, the first on the Western Region. Shorter than a conventional railcar, it ran on four, rather than eight wheels, though seated 46 passengers and allowed space for luggage. The railbuses ran a more intensive service than the steam trains they replaced and also served a new halt opened at Chesterton Lane. To keep costs as low as possible, the platform was at rail level rather than the floor level of the railbus. This new halt proved popular and encouraged BR to open one at Park Leaze.

It had been intended running the railbuses through to Swindon to obviate the tiresome change at Kemble, but this proved impossible as the lightweight vehicle could not be relied on to operate the signalling track circuits on the main line. A railbus sometimes suffered through overcrowding, but this had to be tolerated as its replacement with a larger railcar would have increased operating costs and interfered with the cyclic working in conjunction with the Tetbury branch. The railbuses carried the first conductor/guards on BR — another economy, since it meant that there was no need for booking clerks and ticket collectors at stations. Despite the fact that the branch received considerable support, it was declared uneconomic and closed to passengers on 6 April 1964, closing to goods 18 months later.

Cirencester station, designed by Brunel and R. P. Brereton his resident assistant, is a good example of Victorian Gothic railway architecture carried out in stone. Originally built with a small overall roof, this train shed was removed in 1874, the standard platform canopy replacing it not giving the required balance and making the building appear tall and narrow when viewed from the ends. In 1956 a partial rebuilding took place, H. E. B. Cavanagh taking great care to maintain the original style. Included in the Department of the Environment list of historic buildings, it is now used as a bus station.

Tetbury Branch

Although passengers and goods were conveyed by road between Tetbury Road station and Tetbury itself, this was only a stop-gap measure until a line could be built. In the eighteen-sixties a plan was put forward for extending the Stonehouse & Nailsworth Railway through Tetbury and Malmesbury to the main Great Western line at Christian Malford between Swindon and Chippenham, but this scheme proved abortive. On 28 August 1872, Colonel Nigel Kingscote MP, called a public meeting 'To consider the propriety of taking the necessary steps for obtaining railway communication between the Town of Tetbury and the Great Western Railway near Kemble Junction'. The GWR agreed to purchase 50 per cent of the shares on condition that all property owners agreed to sell the land required without litigation. Although Miss Anna Gordon agreed to a railway crossing her estate from a junction at Tetbury Road, she found the idea of a junction with the main line at Kemble unacceptable. The Great Western continued negotiations with her and an Act authorising the Tetbury branch was passed in 1884.

Announcement in the *Gloucester Journal* 5 June 1841 of the opening of the line to Cirencester.

The extensive timber goods shed at Cirencester *c.* 1900. View towards the terminus. Author's collection

The façade of Cirencester station *c.* 1905. Author's collection

8750 class 0–6–0PT No. 9773 leaves Cirencester Town station for Kemble 21 July 1956. Cattle pens are on the far right and railwaymen's allotments on the left. R. E. Toop

AC Cars railbus W79978 at Cirencester Town, *c.* 1959. It is now preserved. Michael Farr

Chesterton Lane Halt
c. 1961, view Down.
Lens of Sutton

Park Leaze Halt *c.* 1961,
view Up. Lens of Sutton

Park Leaze Halt *c.* 1961,
view Up. Lens of Sutton

The Tetbury branch mixed train 6 September 1952. The Tetbury branch RU (Restricted User) brake van is No. 17390. H. C. Casserley

14XX class 0–4–2T No. 1433 on arrival at Kemble from Tetbury with a mixed train. A bucket for washing hangs on a lamp bracket. Author's collection

16XX class 0–6–0PT No. 1658 heads a train to Tetbury 7 May 1955. A smaller water tank is above the larger. The pumping station is right of the left-hand gantry signal. R. E. Toop

Tetbury to Kemble railbus W79978 at Kemble 5 April 1964 — the last day of service. W79978 has been preserved. Author

Rodmarton Platform.

Church's Hill Halt view Down *c.* 1961. Lens of Sutton

An up mixed train at Culkerton *c.* 1947 hauled unusually by a 45XX class 2–6–2T. Author's collection

Culkerton *c.* 1960 looking very neglected. A footbridge is in the distance. Author's collection

Trouble House Halt, view Up *c.* 1961. Lens of Sutton

Contractors begin preliminary work at the Tetbury station site 1885. Author's collection

A train arrives at Tetbury *c.* 1905. Author's collection

The original timber-built station at Tetbury 1914. Notice the canopy supports. Posters encourage passengers to visit Bath and Weston super Mare. Author's collection

517 class 0–4–2T No. 520 at Tetbury *c.* 1910. No. 520 was withdrawn in October 1912. Author's collection

517 class 0–4–2T No. 520 at Tetbury *c.* 1910. No. 520 was withdrawn in October 1912. Author's collection

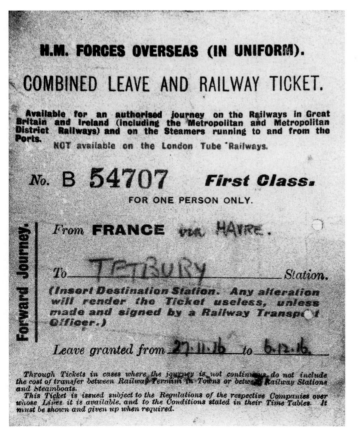

H.M. FORCES OVERSEAS (IN UNIFORM).

COMBINED LEAVE AND RAILWAY TICKET.

Available for an authorised journey on the Railways in Great Britain and Ireland (including the Metropolitan and Metropolitan District Railways) and on the Steamers running to and from the Ports.
NOT available on the London Tube Railways.

No. **B 54707**   **First Class.**
FOR ONE PERSON ONLY.

From **FRANCE** *via* **HAVRE.**

To TETBURY _____ *Station.*
(Insert Destination Station. Any alteration will render the Ticket useless, unless made and signed by a Railway Transport Officer.)

Leave granted from 27.11.16 *to* 6.12.16

Through Tickets in cases where the journey is not continuous do not include the cost of transfer between Railway Termini in Towns or between Railway Stations and Steamboats.
This Ticket is issued subject to the Regulations of the respective Companies over whose Lines it is available, and to the Conditions stated in their Time Tables. It must be shown and given up when required.

Above: The station building at Tetbury before the canopy was extended around all four sides.. Beyond is the goods shed, centre left and the water tank set before the locomotive shed, centre right. Below is a grounded van body. Signs include: Dale Forty Co, pianos; Sutton's Seeds; and Pears' soap. Author's collection

Left: A first class WWI leave ticket from France to Tetbury.

Wagon No. 1 of Charles Hill, Tetbury coal merchant. Coloured purple-brown it was built in April 1897 by the Gloucester Carriage & Wagon Company Limited, to carry a load of 8 tons. Author's collection

74XX class 0–6–0PT (82C Swindon) at Tetbury *c.* 1955. It has probably just run round its passenger coach. Author's collection

The interior of an AC Cars railbus. Notice the 3+2 seating. Author's collection

J. Harris & Co. of Brighton was the contractor appointed for building the line, the first sod being turned at Kemble on 18 October 1887. Just over two years later the line was complete. Festivities began on the morning of 2 December 1889, the first public train being the 7.55 a.m. to Kemble. In the afternoon a train arrived at Tetbury carrying official guests to luncheon at the White Hart. Traffic on the line received a boost when, four weeks later, a cattle market opened at Tetbury. As on the Cirencester branch, railbuses were introduced on 2 February 1959 and although these increased traffic by as much as 150 per cent, the line closed on 6 April 1964, having been closed to freight the previous year.

Footplate Trip on an Auto Train, Gloucester Central to Chalford and Return

On 18 April 1963 the author made a footplate trip on an auto train. Arriving at Gloucester Central, I found 0–4–2T No. 1472 of Gloucester shed, waiting with one coach and a four-wheeled van in bay platform No. 6 with the 10.20 a.m. to Chalford. As I was taking photographs it moved forward to the water column so that its tanks could be replenished. Locomotive Inspector Allen whom I had met previously, strode along the platform and introduced me to Driver Butler and Fireman Bridger. The cab seemed rather small for the four of us. In order that the fireman would have plenty of room to swing his shovel, I took up a vantage point behind the driver and was immediately aware of the fact that the large windows at the front of the cab and the low-set boiler made it an ideal machine for getting a good view of the road ahead.

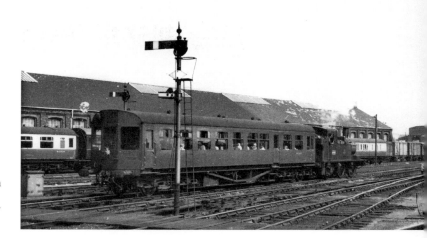

14XX class 0–4–2T No. 1441 leaving Gloucester Central 16 May 1959 with the 2.40 p.m. Saturdays-only Cheltenham St James' to Chalford. R. E. Toop

14XX class 0–4–2T No. 1464 and auto car between duties to Chalford 18 May 1957. R. E. Toop

14XX class 0–4–2T No. 1413 at Gloucester Central 22 June 1952, still in GWR livery. Auto trailer W225 constructed in 1951 is in 'blood and custard' livery. W. Potter

45XX class 2–6–2T No.
4534 and auto trailer pass
Gloucester East signal
box 9 April 1949. No.
4534 retains its buffer
beam number. W. Potter

14XX class 0–4–2T No.
1472 (85B Gloucester
Horton Road) at
Gloucester Central
18 April 1963, being
watered preparatory to
leaving with the 10.20
a.m. to Chalford. The
driver stands ready to
shut off the water supply
when the tanks are filled.
Author

14XX 0–4–2T No. 1472
(85B Gloucester Horton
Road) at Gloucester
Central 18 April 1963,
stands beside Class 5
4–6–0 No. 44822 (17B
Burton on Trent) carrying
express headlights,
waiting to take over a
train. Author

The hand of the pressure gauge pointed to the red arrow showing that the maximum of 165 lb per square inch had been reached. Leaving punctually at 10.20 and clattering over the points, we found the board at Tramway Junction against us for a man was busy cleaning it and the signalman seemed reluctant to disturb him and pull it off. He decided to do so before we had actually stopped. We gathered speed and the driver blew his whistle as he noticed some engine spotters trespassing dangerously near our line. On the outskirts of Gloucester at Quedgeley we were travelling at 41 mph and I observed that No. 1472 had developed a sideways twisting motion. The driver opened the regulator a fraction more and speed rose to 43 mph. At Standish Junction we curved away from the Bristol line and as I glanced down at the fire-hole cover I noticed that it was red hot. We arrived at Stonehouse station two minutes late, overstayed our time and left four minutes behind schedule. At Ebley Crossing Halt we could see Cashes Green Halt ahead, only just over a quarter of a mile distant and two of the closest stations on BR. Passengers took rather longer than the allotted time of half a minute to get on and off, especially those with prams, resulting in us leaving Downfield Halt six minutes late. Fortunately we did not need the seven minutes allowed us at Stroud and after replenishing our tanks and uncoupling the van to be picked up by a shunting engine, we left only one minute behind schedule.

Beyond Stroud the valley became narrower and steeper, the railway continuously curving, flange oilers easing the train round the bends. Before Brimscombe Bridge I noticed some catch points. These are placed near the foot of an incline and set so that a train could go over them in the right direction, but in the event of breakaway, wagons running backwards would be de-railed, thus preventing them striking a following train and causing an accident. At Brimscombe we stopped by the still waters of the Thames & Severn Canal. Leaving only a minute late we passed a banker waiting to give assistance, but with a train of only one coach, we did not require it. We stopped momentarily at St Mary's Crossing Halt, built over the canal. On leaving, No. 1472 worked hard up the steep incline. The ATC siren blew as the Chalford distant signal was on. Rounding the curve we saw that the home signal was off, so we had a clear run into the station. After waiting for the passengers to get out, we drew forward and backed into a siding.

After a while, the train crossed to the Down platform. The coach was now at the leading end of the train. Inspector Allen, Driver Butler and myself walked along the platform and stepped into the driving compartment at the front of the coach, leaving Fireman Bridger alone on the footplate. A passed fireman, he was quite competent to be left by himself and work the necessary controls. An auto train driver depends a great deal on his fireman. In addition to looking after the fire and making sure that there is enough water in the boiler, he is responsible for keeping sufficient vacuum in the pipes to keep the brakes off.

I looked around the driver's vestibule of the auto coach. The regulator handle hung down in front of the middle window and was coupled to the engine by rodding beneath the coach. The whistle was worked by pulling hard on a leather grip round a wire which led over the roof to the locomotive. It was odd seeing the driver pull the whistle and then hearing a distant sound from the rear. A foot operated bell was provided as an additional warning in case the whistle failed to work. A car-type windscreen wiper was provided, but this had to be worked by hand. The guard used an electric bell to signal to the driver to start.

At 11.46 a.m. we left Chalford six minutes late, but I noticed that as we were descending the gradient speed was faster. We arrived at Stroud only five minutes late; however we were delayed an extra three minutes as the shunting engine had to attach a van as tail traffic. The engine was now in the middle of the train — coach first, followed by the locomotive and box van. More time was lost at the halts and

Stonehouse was left nine minutes late leaving us only five minutes to travel the nine miles to Gloucester. The task was an impossible one, but the driver opened the regulator fully. Speed rose to 46 mph and the coach rode very smoothly. At Quedgeley speed had risen to 56 mph. Distants were against us approaching Gloucester, but the home outside the Central station was pulled off just as we approached it. We arrived at 12.28 p.m. — eight minutes late.

Log of Trip on 18th April 1963
Locomotive: 0–4–2T No. 1472 Coaches: 1 + van to Stroud
Average Speed: 26 mph

Distance miles	Scheduled arrival h m s	Actual arrival h m s	Scheduled departure h m s	Actual departure h m s
— Gloucester Central	—	—	10 20 0	10 20 45
9 Stonehouse	—	10 38 35	10 36 0	10 40 17
1¼ Ebley Crossing Hlt		10 43 25	10 40 0	10 43 53
¼ Cashes Green Hlt		10 45 18	10 41 0	10 45 45
½ Downfield Crossing Hlt		10 47 20	10 43 0	10 48 55
¾ Stroud	10 45 0	10 50 10	10 52 0	10 53 00
¾ Bowbridge Crossing Hlt		10 55 03	10 54 0	10 55 13
¾ Ham Mill Crossing Hlt		10 57 20	10 56 0	10 57 28
¾ Brimscombe Bridge Hlt		10 59 42	10 58 0	11 00 03
¾ Brimscombe		11 02 00	11 01 0	11 02 23
½ St Mary's Crossing Hlt		11 04 12	11 03 0	11 04 23
¾ Chalford	11 06 0	11 06 58	—	—

Locomotive: 0–4–2T No. 1472
Coaches: 1 + van from Stroud
Average speed: 29 mph

Distance miles	Scheduled arrival h m s	Actual arrival h m s	Scheduled departure h m s	Actual departure h m s
— Chalford	—	—	11 40 0	11 46 25
¾ St Mary's Crossing		11 48 37	11 42 0	11 48 45
½ Brimscombe		11 50 13	11 44 0	11 50 20
¾ Brimscombe Bridge Hlt		11 52 15	11 46 0	11 52 22
¾ Ham Mill Crossing Hlt		11 54 32	11 49 0	11 54 38
¾ Bowbridge Crossing Hlt		—	11 51 0 (Slowed, but did not stop)	
¾ Stroud	11 53 0	11 58 22	11 55 0	12 03 03
¾ Downfield Crossing Hlt		12 05 01	11 58 0	12 05 25
½ Cashes Green Hlt		12 06 45	12 00 0	12 07 30
¼ Ebley Crossing Hlt		12 08 42	12 01 0	12 09 43
1 ¼ Stonehouse		12 12 45	12 05 0	12 13 55
9 Gloucester Central	12 20 0	12 28 08	—	—

Signal Boxes

Signal Boxes	Opened	Closed	No of levers
Swindon Loco Yard 1	1877	27.1.24	NK
Swindon Loco Yard 2	27.1.24	7.7.68	30
Bremell Sidings	7.11.43	23.6.68	25
Purton 1	By 1884	c. 1901	NK
Purton 2	9.1900	16.8.65	37
Minety & Ashton Keynes 1	By 1884	c. 1904	NK
Minety & Ashton Keynes 2	1905	16.6.68	31
Kemble (East)	By 1884	1928	NK
Kemble (West)	NK	1928	NK
Kemble	1928	29.6.68	69
Coates (Tetbury Rd until 1 May 1908)	By 1884	1.2.23	NK
Coates (second box)	1 2.23	3.3.66	29
Sapperton Tunnel	By 1884	c. 1901	NK
Sapperton Sidings	5.1900	5.10.70	27
Frampton Crossing (1)	By 1884	NK	NK
Frampton Crossing (2)	NK	7.9.65	8
Chalford	NK	13.6.65	20
St Mary's Crossing	NK	5.10.70	—
Brimscombe	By 1884	NK	NK
Brimscombe East	1898	5.10.70	25
Brimscombe West	7.1896	17.5.64	16
Stroud B (later East)	By 1884	10.8.05	NK
Stroud East	10.8.05	5.10.70	41
Stroud A (later West)	NK	25.11.17	NK
Beard's Lane Crossing	By 1884	23.11.58	6
Jefferies' Siding	26.7.1898	1936	13
Stonehouse (1)	By 1884	1922	NK
Stonehouse (2)	1922	5.10.70	40

MR signal boxes controlled line Standish Jc — Tuffley Jc inclusive

Signal Boxes	Opened	Closed	No of levers
Standish Junction(1)	8.7.1844	19.5.1854	NK
Standish Junction(2)	21.4.1873	1887	NK
Standish Junction(3)	25.7.08	14.10.68	NK
Haresfield	NK	15.9.68	NK
Naas Crossing	NK	15.9.68	NK
Tuffley Junction (1)	NK	7.12.41	NK
Tuffley Junction (2)	7.12.41	10.8.68	NK
Gloucester No. 1	By 1884	11.11.01	NK
Gloucester South Jc	11.11.01	25.5.68	71
Gloucester No. 2	By 1884	c. 1901	NK
Gloucester North	4.1901	25.5.68	47
Gloucester East (1)	NK	31.7.31	NK
Gloucester East (2	31.7.31	2.3.68	110
Gloucester Middle	NK	31.7.31	NK
Gloucester West	c. 1892	25.5.68	33

NK = Not known

Bibliography

Locomotive & Train Working in the Nineteenth Century, Vol. 4, E. L. Ahrons, Heffer 1953

Titled Trains of the Western, C. J. Allen, Ian Allan 1974

The Western Since 1948, G. F. Allen, Ian Allan 1979

 Board of Trade Inspectors' Reports

The Cirencester Branch, N. Bray, Oakwood Press 1998

Regional History of the Railways of Great Britain: Vol. 13 *Thames & Severn*, R. Christiansen, David & Charles 1981

An Historical Survey of Selected Great Western Stations, Vol. 1, R. H. Clark, OPC 1976

Closed Stations & Goods Depots, C. R. Clinker, Avon-Anglia 1978

Track Layout Diagrams, Sections 20 & 35, R. A. Cooke 1988; 1978

Railway Motor Buses and Bus Services in the British Isles 1902-1933, Volume 2; J. Cummings, OPC 1980

Tramways of the West of England, P. W. Gentry, LRTL 1960

Canals of South and South East England, C. Hadfield, David & Charles 1969

Industrial Locomotives of Central Southern England, R. K. Hateley, Industrial Railway Society 1981

The Thames & Severn Canal, H. Household, David & Charles 1969

An Historical Survey of Great Western Engine Sheds 1947, E. Lyons PC 1974

An Historical Survey of Great Western Engine Sheds 1837-1947, E. Lyons & E. Mountford, OPC 1979

History of the Great Western Railway, E. T. MacDermot, revised by C. R. Clinker Ian Allan 1964

The Birmingham & Gloucester Railway, C. G. Maggs, Line One 1986

Branch Lines of Gloucestershire, C. G. Maggs Alan Sutton 1991

The Bristol & Gloucester Railway, C. G. Maggs, Oakwood Press 1992

Rail Centres: Swindon, C. G. Maggs, Ian Allan 1983

Railways of the Cotswolds, C. G. Maggs, Peter Nicholson 1981

Swindon to Gloucester, Mitchell V. & Smith K., Middleton Press 2005

Gloucestershire Railway Stations, M. Oakley, the Dovecote Press 2003

The Great Western At Swindon Works, A. S. Peck, OPC 1983

The Works of I. K. Brunel, ed. Sir Alfred Pugsley n.d.

Locomotives of the Great Western Railway, RCTS 1952-1992

The Tetbury Branch, S. Randolph, Wild Swan 1985

Great Western Railway Halts, K. Robertson, Vol. 1 Irwell Press 1990; Vol. 2 KBB Publications 2002

Newspapers & Magazines

Bath Chronicle, Branch Line News, British Railway Journal, Cotswold Life, Engineering, Gloucestershire Countryside, Gloucester Journal, Great Western Railway Magazine, Railway & Travel Monthly, Railway Magazine, Railway Observer, Stroud Journal and *Wilts & Gloucestershire Standard.*